EMPLOYMENT ACT

EXPLANATORY NOTES

INTRODUCTION

1. These explanatory notes relate to the Employment Act 2002, which received Royal Assent on 8th July 2002. They have been prepared by the Department of Trade and Industry (DTI) in order to assist the reader of the Act. They do not form part of the Act and have not been endorsed by Parliament.

2. The notes need to be read in conjunction with the Act. They are not, and are not meant to be, a comprehensive description of the Act. So where a provision does not seem to require any explanation or comment, none is given.

3. Because this Act contains a number of provisions, covering several subject areas, each of the main areas is introduced and described separately in the notes. The section below gives a brief overview of the Act's structure. Certain overarching issues (for example, the Act's financial effects and its impact on public sector manpower) are grouped at the back of the document. Also at the end, there is a glossary of some of the common terms that occur in more than one part of the notes. These terms are underlined wherever they first appear under a heading in the commentary (for example, Statutory Maternity Pay)

OVERVIEW OF THE ACT

4. The main areas covered by the Act are paternity and adoption leave and pay, maternity leave and pay, flexible working, employment tribunal reform and resolving disputes between employers and employees.

5. In many cases the Act amends current legislation. More specifically it amends:

    - The Employment Rights Act 1996 to make provision for statutory rights to paternity and adoption leave and amend the law relating to statutory maternity leave,

    - The Social Security Contribution Benefits Act 1992 to introduce statutory paternity and adoption pay and to amend the law relating to maternity pay and maternity allowance.

    - The Employment Tribunals Act 1996 in relation to costs and expenses, conciliation, powers to delegate the prescription of forms, determination without a hearing, practice directions and pre-hearing reviews,

- The Employment Rights Act 1996 to make provision in connection with the use of statutory procedures in employment disputes, and to introduce a new provision relating to procedural unfairness in unfair dismissal cases. In addition amendments are made to the Act's provisions relating to the particulars of employment that employers are required to give to employees, and to provisions relating to dismissal procedures agreements,

- The Equal Pay Act 1970 to make provision for questionnaires in relation to equal pay issues,

- The Trade Union and Labour Relations (Consolidation) Act 1992 to make provision for time off for trade union learning representatives in organisations where trades unions are recognised, and

- The Social Security Administration Act 1992 to make provision for work-focused interviews for partners of benefit claimants and to make provision about the use of information for, or relating to, employment and training.

6. Sections in the Act relating to pay and administration of statutory paternity and adoption pay, fixed term work, and statutory dispute resolution procedures are free standing and do not amend existing legislation.

COMMENTARY ON SECTIONS

PART ONE: STATUTORY LEAVE AND PAY

Chapter One: Paternity and adoption leave and pay

7. In the 2001 General Election manifesto the Government made a commitment to "help parents devote more time to their children early in life". The Government launched a review of maternity and parental rights in the early summer of 2000. The terms of reference of the review were to "consider the steps needed to make sure that parents have choices to help them balance the needs of their work and their children so that they may contribute fully to the competitiveness and productivity of the modern economy". The review led to the publication of the Green Paper 'Work and Parents: Competitiveness and Choice' in December 2000. The consultation process initiated by the Green Paper closed in early March 2001. Following on from an announcement made by the Prime Minister in the light of the results of the Green Paper consultation, it was announced in the Chancellor's Budget Statement on 7 March 2001 that extensions to maternity and parental rights would be provided. These included the introduction of a new right to two weeks' paid paternity leave, and 26 weeks' paid

adoption leave. All the measures were to be implemented from 2003. Subsequently, the Government published three framework documents[1] taking forward the options for simplification of maternity leave, paternity leave and adoption leave. After the close of the consultation exercise that followed, the Government response to the consultation[2] was published.

8. Sections 1-16 make provision for new rights for paternity and adoption leave and pay. These include:

- Paternity leave following the birth of a child or the placement of a child for adoption. This will be for a period of up to two weeks.

- Adoption leave around the placement of a child for adoption. This will be for a period of up to one year.

- Statutory Paternity Pay for a period of up to two weeks.

- Statutory Adoption Pay for a period of up to 26 weeks.

Paternity leave and Statutory Paternity Pay

9. Since 1999 fathers have been entitled to unpaid parental leave but they have not until now had a statutory right to paid leave to care for a child. Paid paternity leave in some form is offered by many employers - either on an ad hoc basis (as in many small firms) or as a formalised policy for all staff.

10. After the consultation process ended in 2001, the Government announced it was introducing a right to two weeks' paid paternity leave from 2003. The new right to paternity leave is in addition to the right to 13 parental leave weeks' (18 weeks' for parents of disabled children) provided for in regulations made under the Employment Rights Act 1996. Statutory Paternity Pay will be financed by the state, with employers able to recover most or all of the amount of Statutory Paternity Pay they pay out.

---

[1] *Work and Parents: Competitiveness and Choice, a framework for simplification* - published May 2001 (available at http://www.dti.gov.uk/er/review.htm)
Work and Parents: Competitiveness and Choice, a framework for paternity leave - published May 2001 (available at http://www.dti.gov.uk/er/review.htm)
Work and Parents: Competitiveness and Choice, a framework for adoption leave - published May 2001 (available at http://www.dti.gov.uk/er/review.htm)

[2] *Work and Parents: Competitiveness and Choice, Government response on simplification of maternity leave, paternity leave and adoption leave* - published November 2001 (available at http://www.dti.gov.uk/er/review.htm)

Section 1: Paternity leave

11.   This section makes provision for the introduction of a new statutory right to two weeks' paternity leave. Regulations will provide for this to be taken in a single block of either one week or two weeks at the choice of the father. The intention is to make paternity leave available to fathers following the birth of a child or the placement of a child for adoption.

12.   The provisions set out in the section are similar in construction to the provisions in the Employment Rights Act 1996 (ERA) in relation to parental leave, and this section inserts them into the ERA.

13.   Regulations will be made making paternity leave available to an employee:

- who has a relationship (to be specified in regulations) with a newborn child, or a child newly placed for adoption, and has a relationship (to be specified in regulations) with the mother or adoptive parent. It is intended that paternity leave will be available to an employee who expects to be parenting the newborn child or the child placed for adoption;

- who gives appropriate notification;

- who gives his employer a self-certificate to support his entitlement to leave, if requested to do so by his employer.

14.   As it is intended that adoption leave will only be available to one spouse in cases where a married couple adopts a child, paternity leave will be available to the other spouse. For practical reasons there will be slight differences in how paternity leave operates as between those adopting within the UK and those adopting overseas. Provisions for overseas adoptions will be made in regulations.

15.   Paternity leave will be available to an employee who has completed a period of qualifying service. It is intended that the requirement will be continuous service with the same employer for at least 26 weeks by the fifteenth week before the child is expected to be born, or by the week in which an approved match with the child is made. (A match occurs when an approved adoption agency matches an adopter with a child.)

16.   An employee will have the right to return to a job following a period of paternity leave. It is intended that regulations will provide for:

- the right to return to the same job following absence of one week's or two weeks' paternity leave in most cases, and

- protection for employees from detriment and unfair dismissal in connection with paternity leave.

Section 2: Statutory Paternity Pay

17. This section incorporates provisions into the Social Security Contributions and Benefits Act 1992 conferring a new statutory right to Statutory Paternity Pay for fathers following the birth of a child or the placement of a child for adoption. Statutory Paternity Pay is to be paid for a period of two weeks, or if regulations so provide, a period of a week or two periods of a week. Regulations will provide for the father to choose to be paid for a single period of one week or two weeks. Statutory Paternity Pay will generally be payable for paternity leave taken within 56 days of the date on which the child is born or placed for adoption.

18. The rate of Statutory Paternity Pay will be set in regulations. From April 2003 it will be the lesser of £100 per week or 90% of the employee's average weekly earnings.

19. Statutory Paternity Pay will be available to an employee who has met the service qualification (continuous service with the same employer for at least 26 weeks by the fifteenth week before the child is expected to be born or by the week in which an approved match is made with the child; and continuous service from that week up to the child's date of birth or placement), has a relationship (to be specified in regulations) with the child and the mother or adoptive parent, gives appropriate notification, and whose average weekly earnings are equal to or above the Lower Earnings Limit applying to National Insurance Contributions (NICs) (£75 per week from April 2002). For practical reasons there will be slight differences in how paternity leave operates between those adopting within the UK and those adopting overseas. Provisions for overseas adoptions will be made in regulations. It is planned that employees who are entitled to Statutory Paternity Pay will have an obligation to give their employer a self-certificate to support their entitlement to pay (the same self-certificate as for paternity leave).

20. Statutory Paternity Pay will be administered by employers in the same way as Statutory Maternity Pay. Employers will be able to recover a percentage of the amount of Statutory Paternity Pay they pay out (limited in most cases to 92%), with small employers who are entitled to Small Employers' Relief (in 2002/3, those with NICs due in a year of £40,000 or less) able to claim 100% and an added payment (in 2002/3 of 4.5% for Statutory Maternity Pay) to compensate for employers' share of National Insurance Contributions payable in respect of Statutory Paternity Pay. Section 7 of the Act provides for a power to make regulations to enable employers to ask for funding, if necessary in advance, from the Inland Revenue where the amount of Statutory Paternity Pay they have to pay their employees exceeds the amount of tax and NICs or Student Loan deductions that they are due to pay to the Inland Revenue. In certain circumstances where an employer fails to pay Statutory Paternity Pay, the Inland Revenue will become responsible for the payment. Liability will also fall on the Inland Revenue from the first week in which an employer becomes insolvent.

21. The framework for Statutory Paternity Pay is similar to that already in place for Statutory Maternity Pay and Working Families' Tax Credit . The distribution of rights and obligations as between primary and secondary legislation follows the model of the Social Security Contributions and Benefits Act 1992 and Tax Credits Act 1999. As under those Acts, administrative and enforcement powers are conferred on the Inland Revenue. Sections 13 - 15 also provide for the exchange of information about Statutory Paternity Pay between the Inland Revenue, the DTI and other relevant departments.

22. To ensure compliance the sections provide for:

    - Employers to keep appropriate records and to make periodic returns to the Inland Revenue

    - Employers to produce those records for inspection by the Inland Revenue

    - Employers to provide information about entitlement to their employees

    - The Inland Revenue to be able to obtain information from both employers and applicants for Statutory Paternity Pay

    - The Inland Revenue to impose penalties where there is refusal or repeated failure to comply

    - The Inland Revenue to make decisions on entitlement in the event of dispute

    - Appeals against decisions made and penalties awarded to be heard by the Independent Tax Commissioners.

Adoption leave and Statutory Adoption Pay

23. Since 1999 adoptive parents have been entitled to unpaid parental leave but they have not until now had a statutory right to paid leave to care for a child. It is best practice for at least one adoptive parent to spend time at home with the child in the months following placement. Support to adoptive parents is currently offered by about a third of employers. After the consultation process ended in 2001, the Government announced it was introducing a right to 26 weeks' paid adoption leave from 2003.

24. Section 3 inserts provisions into the Employment Rights Act 1996 for an adoptive parent to take adoption leave around the placement of a child for adoption. Paid adoption leave will provide time for the adoptive child and parent to adjust to their new relationships. It is hoped that enabling adoptive parents to spend more time with their child will help reduce the number of disrupted placements. The right to return to a job after adoption leave is also intended to benefit those parents who would prefer to return to the labour market but might otherwise have difficulty doing so. Together, the sections on adoption leave and Statutory Adoption Pay aim to fulfil these objectives.

The new right to adoption leave is in addition to the right to 13 weeks' parental leave (18 weeks for parents of disabled children) provided for in regulations made under the Employment Rights Act 1996. The new right to Statutory Adoption Pay will be financed by the state, with employers able to recover a percentage of the amount of Statutory Adoption Pay they pay out.

Section 3: Adoption leave

25. This section contains provision for a new statutory right to ordinary adoption leave and additional adoption leave for an adoptive parent around the time of placement of a child for adoption. Regulations will determine the entitlement to, and details of, the leave. It is intended that adoption leave will be available whether the child is being adopted within the UK or from overseas. For practical reasons, there will be slight differences to some elements of the provisions for domestic and overseas adoptions. It is intended that ordinary adoption leave will be for a period of up to 26 weeks and additional adoption leave will be for a further period of up to 26 weeks, giving a total of up to one year's leave.

26. The new provisions are framed in a similar way to provisions in the Employment Rights Act 1996 (ERA) in relation to maternity leave, and section 3 inserts them into the ERA.

27. Regulations will be made making adoption leave available:

   - To an adoptive parent who is matched with a child by an approved adoption agency,

   - To employees who give their employer documentary evidence from an approved adoption agency to support their entitlement to leave, if requested to do so by their employer,

   - To both married couples and individuals who adopt,

   - For placements of children up to the age of 18.

28. In cases where a married couple adopts a child, it is planned that only one spouse will be entitled to take the leave. The other spouse will be entitled to two weeks' paternity leave if they meet the qualifying requirements in respect of such leave.

29. Regulations will provide that adoption leave will apply only where the child is newly placed with an adoptive parent - it will not apply to step-family adoptions or adoptions by a child's existing foster carers where there is no placement.

30. Regulations will also provide that adoption leave will be available to an employee who has completed a period of qualifying service. It is intended that the requirement will be continuous service with the same employer for at least 26 weeks by the week

in which an approved match with the child is made (a match occurs when an approved adoption agency matches an adopter with a child).

31.   An employee will have the right to return to a job following a period of adoption leave. It is intended that regulations will allow for:

- the right to return to the same job following absence on ordinary adoption leave in most cases,

- the right to return to the same job, or if that is not reasonably practicable, an appropriate, alternative job, following absence on additional adoption leave, and

- protection for employees from detriment and unfair dismissal in connection with adoption leave.

Section 4: Statutory Adoption Pay

32.   This section contains provisions establishing a new statutory right to Statutory Adoption Pay for adoptive parents around the placement of a child for adoption. Statutory Adoption Pay will be available to an adoptive parent of a child newly placed for adoption - it will not apply to step-family adoptions or adoptions by a child's existing foster carers where there is no new placement - whether the child is being adopted within the UK or from overseas. For practical reasons, there are slight differences to some elements of the provisions for domestic and overseas adoptions. Regulations will set out how Statutory Adoption Pay will apply to overseas adoptions.

33.   New section 171ZN, inserted into the Social Security Contributions and Benefits Act 1992 by section 4, provides that Statutory Adoption Pay will be available for a period of up to 26 weeks. The rate of Statutory Adoption Pay will be set in regulations. From April 2003 it will be the lesser of £100 per week or 90% of the employee's average weekly earnings.

34.   Statutory Adoption Pay will be available to an employee who has met the service qualification (continuous service with the same employer for at least 26 weeks by the week in which an approved match with the child is made), has an approved match with a child, gives appropriate notification, and whose average weekly earnings are equal to or above the lower earnings limit applying to National Insurance Contributions (£75 a week from April 2002). It is planned that employees who are entitled to Statutory Adoption Pay will have an obligation to give their employer documentary evidence from an approved adoption agency to support their entitlement to pay (the same documentary evidence as for adoption leave).

35.   Statutory Adoption Pay will be administered by employers in the same way as Statutory Maternity Pay. Employers will be able to recover a percentage of the amount of Statutory Adoption Pay they pay out (limited in most cases to 92%), with

small employers who are entitled to Small Employers' Relief (in 2002/3, those with NICs due in a year of £40,000 or less) able to claim 100% and an added payment (in 2002/3 of 4.5% for Statutory Maternity Pay) to compensate for employers' share of National Insurance Contributions payable in respect of Statutory Adoption Pay. Section 7 of the Act provides for a power to make regulations to enable employers to ask for funding, if necessary in advance, from the Inland Revenue where the amount of Statutory Adoption Pay they have to pay their employees exceeds the amount of tax and NICs or Student Loan deductions that they are due to pay to the Inland Revenue. In certain circumstances, where an employer fails to pay Statutory Adoption Pay, the Inland Revenue will become responsible for the payment. Liability will also fall on the Inland Revenue from the first week in which an employer becomes insolvent.

36.   The framework for Statutory Adoption Pay is similar to that already in place for Statutory Maternity Pay and Working Families' Tax Credit. The distribution of rights and obligations between primary and secondary legislation is similar to that provided for in the Social Security Contributions and Benefits Act 1992 and Tax Credits Act 1999. As under those Acts, administrative and enforcement powers are to be conferred on the Inland Revenue. Sections 13 - 15 provide for the exchange of information about Statutory Adoption Pay between the Inland Revenue, the DTI and other relevant departments.

37.   To ensure compliance the sections provide for:

- Employers to keep appropriate records and to make periodic returns to the Inland Revenue

- Employers to produce those records for inspection by the Inland Revenue

- Employers to provide information about entitlement to their employees

- The Inland Revenue to be able to obtain information from both employers and applicants for Statutory Adoption Pay

- The Inland Revenue to impose penalties where there is refusal or repeated failure to comply

- The Inland Revenue to make decisions on entitlement in the event of dispute

- Appeals against decisions made and penalties awarded to be heard by the independent Tax Commissioners

Section 17: Maternity Leave

38.   In May 2001, the Secretary of State for Trade and Industry announced that ordinary maternity leave would be increased to 26 weeks, followed by 26 weeks additional

maternity leave, giving most mothers up to one year's maternity leave in total. These changes will be made in regulations.

39.   This section amends Section 71(4) of the Employment Rights Act 1996 to enable the regulations to address the implications of the extension to maternity leave when a woman is returning to work.

Section 18-21 and 48 (see paragraph 142): Maternity Pay

40.   Section 18-21 and 48 (see paragraph 142) make changes to Statutory Maternity Pay and Maternity Allowance as announced in the 2001 Budget in the light of responses to the Green Paper "Work and Parents: Competitiveness and Choice". There are also measures to simplify and clarify the arrangements for women and employers. There are two maternity benefits for pregnant working women. Statutory Maternity Pay (SMP) is administered and paid by employers; Maternity Allowance (MA) is paid by the Department for Work and Pensions (DWP). Both are currently paid for a maximum of 18 weeks.

- SMP is paid to employees who satisfy two basic tests. A woman must have been employed continuously by her employer for at least 26 weeks into the 15th week before the <u>expected week of confinement</u> (EWC); and she must earn on average at or above the <u>Lower Earnings Limit</u> (£75 from April 2002). There are two weekly rates. The higher rate is 90% of the employee's average weekly earnings and is payable for the first six weeks for which SMP is payable. The lower rate is a standard rate (£75 from April 2002) which is reviewed annually and is payable for the remaining weeks of the Maternity Pay Period.

- MA is paid to certain women who do not qualify for SMP, to the self-employed, and to recently employed women. To qualify, they must have been employed or self-employed in at least 26 of the 66 weeks (the test period) ending with the week before the EWC. There are two rates of MA. Women whose average earnings are at least equal to the LEL in force at the beginning of their test period receive standard rate MA (equal to the standard rate of SMP, £75 from April 2002). Women whose average earnings are below that LEL but at least £30 receive 90% of their average weekly earnings (subject to a £75 maximum from April 2002).

41.   There are a small number of women who cannot qualify for SMP if they leave their employment after the 15th week before the EWC but before the SMP payment period can commence (from the 11th week before the EWC unless triggered by earlier childbirth). Prior to a decision of a Social Security Commissioner in 2000 it was always understood that women who left their employment after the 15th week before the EWC for whatever reason, would still receive SMP. However, the Social Security Commissioner determined that if a woman ceased to work for her employer for reasons that were not wholly or partly due to her pregnancy, she would not qualify for SMP. Secondary legislation was introduced in 2000 to restore SMP in many of these

cases but the primary powers were insufficient to restore SMP to those few women who leave work voluntarily for reasons wholly unrelated to their pregnancy. This group, who it was always expected would be entitled to SMP, are therefore currently unable to get SMP.

42.   Employers can recover most of the SMP they pay out by making deductions from their contribution payments made to the Inland Revenue. Where SMP has been paid and the amount of SMP due to be recovered exceeds such contribution payments the employer may apply to the Inland Revenue for payment. Currently the rules restrict recovery to contribution payments and allow payments of any excess only to be refundable in arrears. This is less flexible for employers than the arrangements proposed for adoption and paternity pay, where recovery can be made from other payments due to the Inland Revenue and payment of the excess made in advance.

43.   In summary, the sections increase the standard rate of SMP and MA, extend the payment period, safeguard an employee's entitlement to SMP at the 15th week before the EWC and enable employers to recover SMP in advance and from all payments due to the Inland Revenue. The changes to the rate of SMP and MA will apply to women in receipt of maternity pay on or after 6 April 2003. All other changes will apply to women with an expected week of childbirth beginning on or after 6 April 2003.

44.   In particular, sections 18-21 and 48 (see paragraph 141):

  • Extend the payment period of MA and SMP from 18 to 26 weeks.

  • Allow for an increase in the standard rate of MA and SMP to £100 a week, or 90% of weekly earnings if this is less than £100. In the case of SMP a woman will receive 90% of her average weekly earnings for the first 6 weeks for which SMP is payable (as now).

  • Increase the minimum period of notice that must be given to employers for SMP from 21 days to 28 days.

  • Safeguard an employee's entitlement to SMP from the 15th week before the EWC on her satisfying the employment and earnings tests and giving notice where appropriate. This will be the case even if should happen that, *for whatever reason*, her employment ends after this point.

  • Allow an employer to offset his SMP payments against any payments due to be made to the Inland Revenue as may be prescribed in regulations. Regulations may also provide for employers to apply for advance funding if the amount they are due to pay in SMP will exceed the tax, national insurance and other allowable payments due to be made to the Inland Revenue.

45.   Sections 18-21 and 48 (see paragraph 141) amend sections 35, 35A, 164, 165, 166

and 167 of the 1992 Social Security Contributions and Benefits Act 1992, which contains the rules for Statutory Maternity Pay and Maternity Allowance.

Section 18: Maternity Pay Period

46. This section amends section 165(1) of the Social Security Contributions and Benefits Act 1992 by extending the period of SMP from 18 to 26 weeks.

47. Section 35(2) of the Social Security Contributions and Benefits Act 1992 links the MA period directly to section 165 and hence to the SMP period. Consequently, the period of MA is also extended.

Section 19: Rate of Statutory Maternity Pay

48. This section inserts a new section 166 of the Social Security Contributions and Benefits Act 1992, which sets out the rate of SMP.

49. The inserted section 166(1) provides that, as before, a woman shall be paid at the earnings-related rate (90% of her average weekly earnings) for the first 6 weeks for which it is payable. But this rate is no longer underpinned by the flat rate. For the remaining 20 weeks, the woman will receive a prescribed standard rate (£100 a week) unless this exceeds her earnings-related rate, in which case, she will receive the earnings-related rate for the entire pay period.

> Example:
>
> - Woman **A** earns an average of £200 a week. She therefore receives SMP at £180 for the first 6 weeks, then £100 for the remaining 20 weeks.
>
> - Woman **B** earns an average of £90 a week. She therefore receives SMP at £81 for the whole 26 week period because the earnings-related rate is less that the flat rate.

50. The inserted subsection 166(2) states that (as now) the earnings-related rate is calculated on the basis of average earnings during the 8 weeks immediately preceding the 14th week before the EWC.

51. The inserted subsection 166(3) ensures that (as now) the weekly standard rate must not be less than the weekly rate of Statutory Sick Pay.

Section 20: Entitlement to Statutory Maternity Pay

52. This section amends section 164 of the Social Security Contributions and Benefits Act 1992. Section 164 deals with a woman's entitlement to SMP and employers' liability

to pay it. In particular:

- Paragraph (a) amends section 164(2)(a) of the Act. The amendment does not affect the requirement for a woman to have been employed by her employer for a continuous period of 26 weeks into the 15th week before her expected week of confinement. She must also have ceased to work for him but the requirement that she ceases work "wholly or partly because of pregnancy or confinement" is omitted. This restores the original intention which is to safeguard a woman's entitlement to SMP should her employment end for whatever reason after the beginning of the 15th week.

- Paragraph (b) replaces section 164(4) which sets out the notice a woman is required to give her employer of the start of her maternity pay period. Instead of requiring a woman to give notice of her absence from work because of her pregnancy, she is required to give her employer notice of the date she expects his liability to pay her SMP to start. In addition the minimum notice period is increased from 21 days to 28 days to harmonise with similar changes to maternity leave.

- Paragraphs (c) and (d) provide a power, as now, to modify the entitlement and notice provisions in certain cases; for example early birth.

Section 21: Funding of employers' liabilities: Statutory Maternity Pay

53. Subsection (1) of this section inserts a new section 167 in the Social Security Contributions and Benefits Act 1992, which provides for employers to recover most or all of the Statutory Maternity Pay they have paid out.

54. The inserted section 167, as now, provides for regulations to be made so that employers can recover 92% of the amount paid out by way of Statutory Maternity Pay and for small employers to recover all of the SMP paid out plus an additional amount in compensation for the employers' share of national insurance contributions paid on SMP. As now, the meaning of "small employer" will be defined in regulations by reference to the amount of contribution payments made by an employer.

55. However, subsection (5) of the inserted section 167 provides for regulations to be made so that employers can recover SMP from tax and other payments due to the Inland Revenue and not just from contributions payments as now. In addition regulations will provide for employers to apply for advance payments of SMP if necessary where the amount they have to pay out in SMP exceeds allowable payments due to the Inland Revenue. Regulations (under subsection (5)(c)) will also provide for the Inland Revenue to recover any overpayments generated by such advance payments. This provision aligns SMP recovery with similar provisions being introduced for Statutory Paternity Pay and Statutory Adoption Pay.

56.   Subsection (2) makes corresponding provision for Northern Ireland.

PART 2: TRIBUNAL REFORM

Costs and expenses

57.   The <u>Employment Tribunals Act 1996</u> authorises employment tribunal procedure regulations to provide for the award of costs or expenses (costs are known in Scotland as expenses). The regulations provide that where in the opinion of the tribunal a party has in bringing the proceedings, or a party or his/her representative has in conducting the proceedings, acted vexatiously, abusively, disruptively or otherwise unreasonably, then the tribunal shall consider whether to award costs against that party and may do so. Similarly, costs may be awarded where the bringing or conducting of the proceedings by a party has been misconceived (which includes having no reasonable prospect of success). The regulations do not give tribunals a general power to award costs against the losing party, in the absence of these factors. There will be no change to the circumstances in which the tribunal may award costs against such a party.

58.   As far as the Employment Appeal Tribunal is concerned, the power in the Employment Tribunals Act 1996 to make rules dealing with costs and expenses is limited to cases where the proceedings were unnecessary, improper or vexatious or there has been unreasonable delay or other unreasonable conduct in bringing or conducting the proceedings.

59.   In its consultation document 'Routes to Resolution', the Government suggested "all concerned - users, their representatives and the tribunals - must play their part in ensuring that time wasting is minimised." Specifically, the document proposed giving the tribunals new powers to make orders for wasted costs against representatives are acting on a for profit basis; changing the presumption on costs; and allowing any costs awarded to include the time spent preparing the case. Currently employment tribunals cannot include in any award an amount to reflect time spent by a party preparing for the employment tribunal claim and there is no power to make an award directly against a representative, where his/her behaviour has been found inappropriate

Section 22: Awards of costs or expenses against representatives

60.   This section extends the scope for making employment tribunal procedure regulations set out in section 13 of the Employment Tribunals Act 1996 (costs and expenses). It does this by substituting subsection (1) of section 13 with four subsections.

61.   Specifically, the amendment gives the Secretary of State power by regulations to authorise tribunals to make awards of costs directly against a party's representative, because of the way the representative has conducted the proceedings. The award could mean that the representative may not recover his/her fees from the client, or that he/she has to pay costs incurred by the client, or costs incurred by the other party, as a

result of his/her misconduct. It is intended that the regulations will include safeguards to allow the representative the opportunity to put his/her case on any proposed award. The regulations will also be able to define "representative" so as to exclude the not-for-profit sector from wasted costs orders.

Section 22: Payments in respect of preparation time

62.   This section also inserts a new section 13A into the Employment Tribunals Act 1996. It gives the Secretary of State power by regulations to authorise tribunals to order that one party make a payment to the other in respect of the time spent in preparing the other party's case. It is not intended that the parties should have to provide detailed evidence of the actual time they have spent preparing for a case, but that the tribunal should make an assessment based on guidelines to be set out in the <u>Employment Tribunal Rules of Procedure</u>. It is intended that the new awards could be made only in the circumstances in which a costs award may be made at present, that is, where the party's case is misconceived, or they or their representative have behaved vexatiously, abusively, disruptively or otherwise unreasonably.

63.   The new section 13A provides that the regulations on costs and preparation time must include a provision that the tribunal may not make an award of both costs and preparation time in favour of the same person in the same proceeding.

64.   The amendments made by section 22 also contain specific powers for the procedure regulations to allow tribunals to take into account a party's ability to pay when making a costs or preparation time award. This is because a recent Court of Appeal decision in *Kovacs v Queen Mary & Westfield College and the Royal Hospitals NHS Trust* ruled that a tribunal may not take into account a party's ability to pay when making a costs award. The Government believes that the tribunal should have the discretion to consider a party's means, where appropriate. This will be given effect in the regulations.

Section 23: Costs and expenses in the Employment Appeal Tribunal

65.   This section replaces the existing section 34 of the Employment Tribunals Act 1996, which deals with costs in the Employment Appeal Tribunal. The power is aligned with the power to make costs rules for employment tribunals. Thus the power to make rules for the EAT is no longer limited to certain types of case, there is provision for wasted costs orders against representatives and specific provision for taxation or detailed assessment of costs. The rules will set out the limited circumstances in which costs orders can currently be made in the Employment Appeal Tribunal (see paragraph 58 above). The new section 34 also provides for the Employment Appeal Tribunal rules to enable the EAT to take into account a party's ability to pay when making a costs award.

Miscellaneous

Conciliation

66. The Advisory Conciliation and Arbitration Service's (ACAS) present role is, among other things, to provide an independent and impartial service to prevent and resolve disputes between employers and employees. ACAS conciliators currently have a statutory duty to promote settlements of a wide range of employment rights complaints, which have been made or could be made to an employment tribunal. Section 24 establishes a fixed period of conciliation for claims to the employment tribunal.

Section 24: Fixed period of conciliation

67. At present, ACAS has a duty to continue to seek a conciliated settlement between the employer and employee for as long as the two parties to the dispute want to carry on. This can sometimes lead to an ACAS-brokered settlement being reached at the very last moment before the case comes before an employment tribunal. The Government believes that on occasions this is the result of the parties being unwilling to focus on the importance of agreement until the reality of the tribunal hearing is upon them. But delayed settlements cost time and resource to the parties involved, to ACAS and to the tribunal services. The objective, therefore, is to introduce a system that encourages earlier conciliated settlement where this is possible, without preventing last minute settlements if there is good reason for them.

68. This section therefore provides a power for the employment tribunal procedure regulations to introduce a fixed period for conciliation. This is achieved by amending section 7 of the Employment Tribunals Act 1996 to allow for regulations to be made enabling the postponement of the fixing of a time and place for a hearing in order for the proceedings to be settled through conciliation. It is intended that the regulations will set out the length of the conciliation period and will provide for its extension only in cases where the conciliator considers that settlement within a short additional timeframe is very likely.

69. The section provides that ACAS's duty to conciliate cases reverts to a power to conciliate after the conciliation period has ended. This preserves ACAS's conciliation role in all of the jurisdictions for which it currently has a duty to act, but means that once the conciliation period is over, this duty becomes a power. The effect will be that once the conciliation period is over, the conciliation officer can judge whether to continue to conciliate the case, or to pass it back to the Employment Tribunal Service (ETS) so that a time and place can be fixed for a hearing.

Section 25: Power to delegate prescription of forms etc.

70. Section 7(2) of the Employment Tribunals Act 1996 provides that proceedings must be instituted in accordance with employment tribunal procedure regulations.

Currently, the main Employment Tribunal Rules of Procedure stipulate that tribunal applications must be in writing and include the applicant's and respondent's details and the grounds on which relief is sought. A respondent's notice of appearance must be in writing and must give the respondent's details, state whether or not he intends to resist the application and if so, the grounds for doing so. The ETS produces two forms, one for use as an originating application (IT1) and one for use as a notice of appearance (IT3). However, the forms have no particular status under the rules.

71.   This section amends section 7 of the Employment Tribunals Act 1996 by inserting a new subsection (3ZA). It provides a power for the rules to delegate to the Secretary of State the authority to prescribe a form, which is required to be used to institute proceedings in a tribunal. Alternatively, the section enables the Secretary of State to include the requirements of the form partly in the rules and partly outside the rules. (Existing powers would enable a form to be prescribed in the rules themselves). The same powers apply in relation to the appearance to be entered by the respondent to the proceedings. It is anticipated that the mandatory form and notice will provide more information to the tribunal, and to the other side, at an earlier stage. This will help the tribunal in deciding whether the application would benefit from a pre-hearing review, preliminary consideration or case management hearing, and the length of time required for the hearing. An assessment of the strength of the other side's case could also be made, which could encourage settlement. The section also enables the rules to delegate to the Secretary of State the power to prescribe that certain documents (such as the written statement of particulars of employment) must accompany either form.

72.   Finally, the section enables the rules to include provision to ensure the publication of any requirements prescribed by the Secretary of State by virtue of this section.

Section 26: Determination without a hearing

73.   This section provides for employment tribunal procedure regulations to authorise cases to be determined without a hearing in the circumstances prescribed by the regulations. It is intended that the circumstances in which a case may be determined in this way would be where both parties have given their consent, by signing a form waiving their rights to an oral public hearing, following independent advice. This would be subject to the tribunal deciding that there should be an oral public hearing notwithstanding the parties' agreement to the contrary. This is achieved by substituting a new subsection (3A) for the existing subsection (3A) in section 7 of the Employment Tribunals Act 1996.

Section 27: Practice directions

74.   Unlike the President of the Employment Appeal Tribunal (EAT), the Employment Tribunal Presidents do not have the power to issue practice directions. That was confirmed by the EAT in the case of *Eurobell Holdings Plc v Barker*. However, the EAT noted that it was undesirable that employment tribunals should adopt different practices and procedures in different regions and that, if need be, the President should

be given statutory power to make practice directions which apply countrywide. It was noted in the 1994 Green Paper 'Resolving Employment Disputes – Options for Reform' that some tribunal chairmen favoured the issuing of formal practice directions by Tribunal Presidents, to guide them on how discretions ought to be exercised. Examples of such discretions include rule 4 of the main Employment Tribunal Rules of Procedure, which says that a tribunal *may* issue directions, or rule 17 where it *may* extend certain time limits.

75. By providing Tribunal Presidents with the power to issue practice directions, the Government's objective is to ensure that tribunals adopt a consistent approach to procedural issues and to the interpretation of their powers under the Employment Tribunal Rules of Procedure. It is believed that such consistency will lead to an increase in confidence among users of the tribunal system that cases are being dealt with in a uniform way regardless of where they are heard.

76. This section inserts a new section 7A into the Employment Tribunals Act 1996, giving a power to amend the employment tribunal procedure regulations so that Tribunal Presidents can issue practice directions. There are currently two Presidents in Great Britain – one for England and Wales and one for Scotland. The Presidents will be able to issue these directions in respect of Employment Tribunal Rules of Procedure and the exercise by tribunals of powers under them. In addition, the procedure regulations may contain provisions about securing compliance with practice directions and their publication. The procedure regulations may also refer to provision made or to be made by practice directions, instead of making such provision themselves.

Section 28: Pre-hearing reviews

77. Employment tribunals may currently carry out preliminary considerations (pre-hearing reviews) and if it is found at the review that the party's case has no reasonable prospect of success, a deposit of up to £500 can be required as a condition of proceeding to a full hearing. Only on refusal to pay the deposit can the case be struck out. Although rule 4 and 15 of the main Employment Tribunal Rules of Procedure permits the strike out of proceedings in certain circumstances, it is arguable that these do not apply to the pre-hearing review stage.

78. At present the power to strike out is limited and rarely used. This section therefore clarifies that rules may permit tribunals to strike out a case at the pre-hearing review on grounds which do not go beyond those applicable to other stages of proceedings. Such grounds include when the originating application or notice of appearance (or anything in it) is scandalous, misconceived or vexatious. The objective is to limit the number of such cases reaching a full hearing by confirming the tribunals' power to strike cases out at this stage in the process. The aim is to improve the efficiency of case handling and restrict the amount of time that tribunals spend on considering cases which are obviously misconceived etc. However, the power to demand a deposit remains and is likely to continue to be the main sanction used against weak cases at

pre-hearing reviews.

79. Examples of cases where it could be appropriate to exercise the strike out power include:

- Cases in which the facts have already been litigated and the applicant has no fresh or different evidence but insists on pursuing the case;

- Cases where the facts are not in dispute, but the interpretation placed on those facts by one party is clearly wrong;

- Cases in which a party's application is not itself sufficient to lead to a successful outcome for him, and the party has stated at the pre-hearing review that no further evidence or witnesses would be called.

80. As the sanctions of imposing a deposit or making a costs order are also available, the power to strike out will only be used where it is appropriate. Since evidence is not considered at the pre-hearing review, the strike-out option will only be appropriate in cases where the tribunal is satisfied that there is no need to consider the evidence, or where there is no conflict of evidence.

81. This section amends section 9 of the Employment Tribunals Act 1996. It works by removing from section 9(1)(a) the implication that pre-hearing reviews are "preliminary" hearings, and therefore necessarily followed by a full hearing. It makes it clear that a pre-hearing review will not necessarily be preliminary, so that the powers which the tribunal can exercise in connection with the pre-hearing review may include a power to strike out the claim. It also provides that a tribunal may not strike out at a pre-hearing review on grounds which do not apply outside such a review

PART 3: DISPUTE RESOLUTION ETC.

Statutory Procedures

82. Around 90% of larger employers have disciplinary and grievance procedures in place. Most are written and included directly or indirectly in employees' contracts. Under a disciplinary procedure, an employer can complain to an employee about his conduct or performance. Sometimes, such procedures are termed "dismissal procedures" where they deal with complaints or issues that can lead to the dismissal of an employee. Grievance procedures operate in the opposite direction and deal with formal complaints initiated by an employee against his employer.

83. Under current law, employment tribunals consider the existence and use of disciplinary procedures in unfair dismissal cases. A failure by an employer to use procedures appropriately can result in a determination by a tribunal that a dismissal was unfair. Tribunals must also take account of the ACAS Code of Practice on

Discipline and Grievance Procedures and any internal procedures the employer may have, when determining the reasonableness or otherwise of the employer's decision to dismiss. The use of procedures can also affect the size of an award an employee may receive when unfairly dismissed. Under section 127A of the Employment Rights Act 1996, if a dismissal is found to be unfair a tribunal has the power to make a supplementary award of up to two weeks' pay where the employer prevented the employee from appealing against dismissal under the employer's procedure. Conversely, where an employee does not utilise the employer's appeal procedure the tribunal has the power to reduce any award by up to two weeks' pay.

84.   Grievance procedures have no equivalent role under current law and employment tribunals do not generally take their use into account in determining complaints under their various jurisdictions. However, under section 10 of the Employment Relations Act 1999, a worker is entitled to be accompanied by a fellow worker or a trade union official at hearings held under a grievance procedure, provided the grievance is non-trivial in nature. Section 10 also provides for a similar right to be accompanied at hearings during disciplinary procedures.

85.   Section 29-34 will bring in:

- Provisions setting out statutory dismissal and disciplinary procedures (DDPs) and statutory grievance procedures (GPs).

- Powers to make these statutory procedures an implied term of all contracts of employment.

- Provisions to enable tribunals to vary compensatory awards by up to 50% where the employer or the applicant has failed to use the minimum statutory procedures. The provisions contain powers enabling the Secretary of State to specify by regulation how the statutory procedures will apply for these purposes. These provisions will in effect replace section 127A of the 1996 Act, which will be repealed.

- Provisions preventing certain categories of complaint from being presented to tribunals until Step 1 of the grievance procedures has been completed and at least 28 days have elapsed thereafter.

- Powers to extend, and to enable employment tribunals to extend, the time limits within which claims need to be made, to allow the relevant statutory procedures to be completed.

- Provisions which will make it unfair for employers to dismiss an employee without meeting their obligations under the relevant DDP. They will also ensure that tribunals disregard any failures by an employer to take other procedural actions outside the framework of the statutory procedure, if taking such additional procedural actions would have had no effect on the decision to dismiss.

- The affirmative resolution procedure applies to the making of all regulations under these sections.

86. A large proportion of complaints to employment tribunals involve employers without any internal disputes procedures. Many occur where employers or applicants have failed to use whatever procedures exist. Litigation to resolve employment disputes is costly and can often weaken employment relations and the employability of applicant workers. These provisions aim to encourage parties to avoid litigation by resolving differences through the proper use of internal procedures. They will, in effect, require all employers to have minimum procedures and give incentives to both employers and employees to use them.

- Section 29 and Schedule 2 - *Schedule 2* specifies the statutory DDP and GP procedures. Under both types of procedures, there is a 3 step standard procedure involving meetings to consider complaints and appeal processes. The Schedule also specifies a short modified version of the DDP and the GP involving just two written steps. Section 29 introduces the Schedule and contains provisions enabling the Secretary of State to amend these statutory procedures by order, following consultations with ACAS.

- Section 30 makes it an implied term of every contract of employment between an employer and an employee that a statutory procedure is to apply in circumstances specified by the Secretary of State in regulations. The section prevents employers and employees from contracting out of this implied term.

- Section 31 and Schedule 3 - Section 31 contains provisions requiring employment tribunals to vary compensatory awards for failures to use the statutory procedures before applications are made to employment tribunals. Unless there are exceptional circumstances, the variation must range between 10% and 50% of the award. However, in exceptional circumstances where a variation on that scale would be unjust or inequitable, tribunals may vary the award by less than 10% or they may decide to make no variation at all. Where an award falls to be adjusted under this section and section 38 the adjustment under this section is to made first. *Schedule 3* lists the jurisdictions covered by the section. Together, the listed jurisdictions cover the overwhelming majority of tribunal claims. Section 31 also gives powers to the Secretary of State to add or remove jurisdictions from the list. The section also gives the Secretary of State powers to make provision as to how the statutory procedures will apply for these purposes. These powers enable the Secretary of State in particular to specify circumstances where an employee or an employer is to be treated as having complied with a statutory procedure, even though none or only some of the required actions have been taken. In other words, the regulations could provide for exemptions from some of the requirements of the statutory procedures in particular circumstances.

- Section 32 contains provisions preventing certain categories of complaint from being presented to tribunals until Step 1 of the grievance procedures has been completed and at least 28 days have elapsed thereafter. The section also gives the Secretary of State powers to make provision about the application of the grievance procedure and what constitutes compliance.

- Section 33 gives the Secretary of State the power to make regulations about the time limits for beginning certain proceedings in an employment tribunal. In particular, regulations may cover extending the time for beginning proceedings, the exercising of discretion to extend the time for the beginning of proceedings and treating proceedings begun out of time as having been begun within time. The purpose of the powers is to allow time for the relevant statutory procedure to be completed before a complaint has to be presented to a tribunal.

- Section 34 - Currently, if an ex-employee complains to a tribunal that he has been unfairly dismissed, then the former employer needs to meet two tests in order to show that the dismissal was fair. First, he must show that the reason for the dismissal was one of the five reasons, which count as potentially fair reasons for dismissal (as set out in sections 98(1) and (2) of the Employment Rights Act 1996). Second, the dismissal itself must be reasonable in the circumstances. This second point has given rise to a large amount of complex and sometimes controversial case law around the question of whether or not the employer has to have followed internal disciplinary procedures in order to establish reasonableness. This culminated in a House of Lords decision (Polkey vs A E Dayton Services Ltd, 1988) reversing earlier case law which said, in effect, that if an employer failed to follow appropriate disciplinary procedures before dismissal, then he generally cannot justify this on the basis that it would have made no difference to his decision to dismiss if that procedure had been followed. It has been argued that this judgment, by removing the so-called 'no difference' test, forces tribunals to put undue weight on questions of disciplinary procedure, rather than on the actual reasons for the dismissal.

- The Government consulted in the 'Routes to Resolution' document and in its reply to the consultation, the Government confirmed that in the light of representations it had received, it intended 'to act to ensure that tribunals disregard procedural mistakes, beyond the statutory minimum procedures, in unfair dismissal cases, if following full procedures would have made no difference to the outcome.'

- Section 34 achieves this by inserting a new Section 98A into the Employment Rights Act 1996. The new section contains provisions that oblige tribunals to disregard failures by employers to take procedural actions outside the framework of the relevant DDP, provided that following such additional procedural actions would have had no effect on the decision to dismiss. The new section would, however, make it unfair for an employer to dismiss an employee without meeting their obligations under the relevant DDP, and provides that an employee will generally receive a minimum of four weeks pay as compensation where they are found to have been unfairly dismissed and the DDP has not been complied with.

Employment Particulars

Sections 35-38: Changes to written statements of terms and conditions

87. Currently, an employer is obliged to provide a new employee with details of their main terms and conditions not later than two months after the employee starts work with the employer. The details, which are set out in sections 1 to 7 of the Employment Rights Act 1996, must cover a number of specified areas such as the name of the employer, the date the employment began and details of disciplinary and grievance procedures applicable to the employee. A further statement must be served if the details change. On the question of disciplinary and grievance procedures, employers with fewer than twenty employees need currently only say to whom the employee can apply for redress of any grievance relating to his employment and the manner in which such an application should be made. Where employees are not issued with a statement of initial employment particulars, or a subsequent change, they can apply to an employment tribunal to determine which particulars ought to have been included or referred to. There is currently no other sanction for failure to provide the required statement.

88. The Government explained in the 'Routes to Resolution' consultation document that it considers the written particulars of the terms and conditions of employment ("the written statement") to be a record of the basis of the employment relationship, and the first point of reference when disputes arise. As such, it has a key role to play in better dispute resolution. A number of changes are therefore to be made to the legislation relating to the written statement, with the object of:

- ensuring that all employers recognise the value of the statement to both themselves and their employees;

- making the content of the statement consistent across employers of all sizes;

- ensuring the statement reflects the Act's requirements for minimum statutory internal discipline and grievance procedures;

- creating a more effective penalty for failing to supply a statement; and

- providing more flexibility to employers in how they go about providing the required statement.

89.   To achieve these objectives, sections 35 to 38 make the following changes:

- Section 35 provides for the part of the written statement dealing with disciplinary and grievance matters to cover the procedure which applies when an employee is dismissed or disciplined, whereas at present it must only describe what he must do if he is dissatisfied with disciplinary action taken against him. This ensures that all stages of the new minimum disciplinary and dismissal procedures must be set out in the written statement.

- Section 36 removes the current exemption, relating to the need for details of disciplinary rules and procedures, for employers with less than 20 employees. This means that all employers of whatever size will have to mention their disciplinary rules and the new minimum procedures in the written statement.

- Section 37 provides flexibility for employers by allowing particulars included in a copy of the contract of employment or letter of engagement given to the employee to form, or to form part of the written statement; this reduces the need for employers to duplicate existing documents. It also enables such documents to be given to the employee before his employment begins.

- Section 38 provides for employment tribunals to award compensation to an employee where the lack, incompleteness or inaccuracy of the written statement becomes evident upon a claim being made under specified tribunal jurisdictions (which cover the main areas such as unfair dismissal, and all types of discrimination – see Schedule 5). This is done by requiring the tribunal to increase any award made against the employer in respect of the complaint under the other jurisdiction by 2 or 4 weeks pay, or to award 2 or 4 weeks pay where compensation is not a remedy available for the particular complaint or where it is not the remedy that the tribunal chooses. Whether to award 2 or 4 weeks pay is a matter for the tribunal's discretion. No award need be made or increased if the tribunal considers that to do so would be unjust or inequitable.

90.   For the most part these changes are brought about by means of amendments to the current provisions relating to written statements.

PART 4: MISCELLANEOUS AND GENERAL

Miscellaneous

Section 42: Equal pay questionnaire

91.   A 'questionnaire' procedure is currently available in individuals' disputes over matters of sex, race and disability discrimination, but not in the area of equal pay

disputes. The procedure has proved useful in discrimination claims, since it assists applicants to set out their cases with the key facts. The question and answer format can help to identify whether the case is weak or strong. The process is familiar to tribunals, as the procedure has been in place for some time under the Sex Discrimination Act 1975, the Race Relations Act 1976, and the Disability Discrimination Act 1995.

92. The proposal to introduce a questionnaire procedure into the Equal Pay Act 1970 (EqPA) was included in the consultation document "Towards Equal Pay for Women" (December 2000) which set out proposals to speed up and simplify equal pay employment tribunal cases. On 8 May Tessa Jowell, then Minister for Women, announced that the Government planned to legislate in this area.

93. Equal pay claims are dealt with under the EqPA, which effectively implements the Equal Pay Directive. The introduction of an equal pay questionnaire to provide a procedure in equal pay disputes will include: prescribed forms, questions and answers as case evidence, a time period for serving questions, and the manner in which these questions and answers can be served.

94. The objective is to bring the questionnaire procedure currently available in disputes over matters of sex, race and disability discrimination, into the area of equal pay disputes. The questionnaire enables the key facts to be settled early, and can encourage not only the establishment of evidence, but also the settlement of cases before they proceed to tribunal.

95. This section inserts a new section 7B in the EqPA, which brings about the following:

- The Secretary of State is given the power to prescribe forms that may be used both by the claimant or potential claimant and by the respondent or potential respondent.

- The questions and replies can be admitted as evidence in subsequent tribunal proceedings, subject to any other rules relating to evidence before the tribunal. The questions and replies may be admitted in evidence whether or not they are in the form prescribed by the Secretary of State. This is the same as in sex and race discrimination questionnaires, as opposed to disability discrimination questions and replies, which can only be admitted in evidence if they are made in the prescribed form.

- The Secretary of State is provided with the power to prescribe, by order, a time period within which questions must be served in order to be admissible as evidence in tribunal proceedings. This is intended to encourage the applicant to pursue a case swiftly.

- If the tribunal considers that the respondent deliberately, and without reasonable excuse, failed to reply within a period prescribed by order, it can draw any inference it considers just or equitable. The tribunal can also draw such an inference if it considers that the respondent's reply was evasive or equivocal. The existing questionnaire procedures under the other discrimination Acts refer to a response within a 'reasonable time'. By contrast, this section allows the Secretary of State to prescribe a time within which a response should be given, which is intended to provide greater certainty for parties and tribunals. At present the intention is to make this eight weeks, but by providing a power to prescribe the period, it can be changed in the future as appropriate. Where the respondent has failed to reply within the prescribed period, the tribunal is only allowed to draw inferences if that failure was deliberate and without reasonable excuse. The respondent therefore has the opportunity to explain if, in the circumstances, he had a reasonable excuse for failing to reply. This is designed to ensure that the provision does not operate unfairly for respondents.

- The Secretary of State is given the power to prescribe the manner in which any question and reply may be duly served. Consideration may well be given to the option of providing that service electronically.

96.   An order under this section is subject to the negative procedure.

Section 43: Union Learning Representatives

97.   Union learning representatives (ULRs) are a new type of lay union representative, whose main function is to advise union members about their training, educational and developmental needs. There are currently around 3,000 ULRs in existence. Their advice is usually provided direct to union members at their place of work, sometimes through face-to-face meetings with individuals.

98.   Under section 168 of the Trade Union and Labour Relations (Consolidation) Act 1992 (the "1992 Act"), officials of an independent trade union which is recognised by their employer for collective bargaining purposes are permitted reasonable time off during working hours to carry out certain trade union duties or to undergo training relevant to carrying out their trade union duties. An employer who permits officials to take such time off must pay them for the time off taken in accordance with section 169 of the 1992 Act. The definition of an "independent union" is provided in section 5 of the 1992 Act.

99.   Section 170 of the 1992 Act provides for employees to take reasonable time off during working hours to take part in the activities of their union. This right applies only where the employees belong to an independent union which is recognised by their employer and they form part of the bargaining unit for which the union is recognised. Employers are not required to pay their employees when they permit them to take this time off.

100.   Employees may present a claim to an employment tribunal where their employer has

failed to provide time off in accordance with sections 168, 169 or 170. Under section 172 of the 1992 Act, the employment tribunal may award compensation to employees where it finds that their complaints are well-founded. Under section 199(2)(a) and (2)(b) of the 1992 Act, the Advisory, Conciliation and Arbitration Service (ACAS) has a duty to provide practical guidance on the time off for trade union duties and activities to be permitted by an employer. In consequence, ACAS has produced a Code of Practice entitled "Time Off for Trade Union Duties and Activities: ACAS code of practice 3". Where relevant, this Code must be taken into account by employment tribunals when determining complaints.

101.   There is no current legislation, which specifically governs the activities of ULRs. ULRs do not fall within the definition of the term "official" used in section 168. It is also unclear whether accessing the services of a ULR falls within the definition of "trade union activities" used in section 170. This means that trade union members have no clear statutory entitlement for time off to undertake the duties of a ULR, to be trained as a ULR or to access the services of a ULR. In effect, it is entirely or largely a voluntary matter whether employers permit ULRs to function at their workplaces and, where they do permit them to function, it is a matter for the employer to decide what time off, if any, is allowed.

102.   The section amends the 1992 Act and provides paid time off rights to ULRs to carry out their functions and undergo training which are broadly equivalent to the current rights enjoyed by trade union officials under section 168. The section amends section 170 to make it clear that the right to unpaid time off under that section applies to union members accessing the services of a ULR. The section also gives powers to ACAS and the Secretary of State to issue a Code of Practice providing practical guidance on the application of these entitlements to reasonable time off.

103.   Subsections (2) And Paragraphs 18, 19 and 20 of Schedule 6

- Subsection (2) inserts a new section 168A into the 1992 Act which specifies the rights to time off for ULRs. This new section has a similar structure to the existing s168 and, in some places, common wording is used.

104.   New Section 168A

- Subsection (1) of new section 168A sets out the general requirement for an employer to allow time off to a ULR. It limits the requirement to ULRs who are members of an independent union recognised by that employer for collective bargaining purposes.

- Subsection (2) defines the activities of a ULR for which time off must be allowed. Together with *subsection (10)*, it limits the time off requirement to activities undertaken on behalf of fellow employees who are members of the

ULR's union and for whom the ULR has the function of acting as a ULR. These employees are categorised as "qualifying members of the trade union". ULRs are therefore not entitled to time off to provide similar services on behalf of non-union members or members of other unions.

- Subsection (3) states that in order for an employee to be entitled to time off, the union must have first notified the employer in writing that the employee is a ULR and has met the training condition.

- Subsection (4) defines the training condition. It requires the employee to be sufficiently trained to carry out his duties either at the time he begins functioning as a ULR or within 6 months of that date. In the latter case, the union must notify the employer in writing or by other means when the employee has received the required training within the six month period. This arrangement allows an insufficiently trained person to function as a ULR for what amounts in effect to a maximum six month probationary period until he receives the required training. If, however, the person does not receive the required training within the six month period, his entitlement to time off ends.

- Subsection (5) prevents the union avoiding this consequence by the device of issuing further notices to the employer, which would in effect establish a new six month probationary period.

- Subsection (6) provides for any relevant Code of Practice issued by ACAS or the Secretary of State to be taken into account in determining what constitutes sufficient training.

- Subsection (7) provides ULRs with a right to time off for training relevant to their functions.

- Subsection (8) restricts a ULR's time off to that which is reasonable in the circumstances, having regard to any relevant Code of Practice issued by ACAS or the Secretary of State. This therefore enables employers to deny a ULR's request for time off where they have good grounds for doing so, provided they act in accordance with any relevant Code.

- Subsection (9) defines that complaints about alleged breaches of a ULR's time off rights are to be determined by employment tribunals. Paragraph 18 of Schedule 6 has the effect (by amendment of section 171 of the 1992 Act) that such complaints must be made within three months of the failure occurring or at an appropriate later date where the employment tribunal is satisfied that a complaint could not have been made within 3 months. Paragraph 19 of Schedule 6 has the effect (by amendment of section 172 of the 1992 Act) that an employment tribunal may make a declaration and award compensation where the employer failed to permit paid time off in accordance with the new section 168A. Paragraph 21 of Schedule 6 has the effect (by amendment of section 18(1)(b) of the Employment Tribunals Act 1996) of providing for ACAS conciliation in any complaints to employment tribunals under this new jurisdiction.

- Subsection (11) provides that a person is a ULR of a trade union for the purposes of the new section if he is appointed or elected as such in accordance with its rules.

- *Subsection (3)* has the effect (by amendment of section 169 of the 1992 Act) of providing for ULRs to be paid for time off taken in accordance with the new section 168A.

- *Subsections (4) and (5)* provide for certain union members to have reasonable time off without pay to access the services of any ULR whose function is to carry out ULR activities in relation to them. This right only applies where the ULR is himself entitled to time off under new section 168A to provide services to such members. It achieves this by amending section 170 of the 1992 Act. This right is enforceable via the employment tribunals.

- *Subsection (6) and Paragraph 20 of Schedule 6* - Section 173 of the 1992 Act currently contains interpretative and supplementary provisions relating to the rights to time off for trade union duties and activities. *Paragraph 20 of Schedule 6* applies the same provisions to new section 168A. *Subsection (6)* inserts new subsections into s173 which make provision for the Secretary of State to amend Section 168A by a statutory instrument under the affirmative resolution procedure changing the purposes for which ULRs are entitled to take time off.

- *Subsection (7)* enables ACAS and the Secretary of State to issue Codes of Practice containing practical guidance on the application of the new statutory entitlements relating to ULRs. ACAS could provide such guidance by amending its current Code of Practice on time off for trade union duties and activities. *Subsection (8)* ensures any draft ACAS Code in this area is approved by each House of Parliament by the affirmative resolution procedures.

- *Paragraph 30 of Schedule 6* amends Section 104 of the Employment Rights Act 1996 to make the dismissal of an employee unfair if the reason for it was that he brought proceedings to enforce a right to time off under the new section 168A or alleged that his employer had infringed such a right.

Section 44: Dismissal Procedures Agreement

105. Section 110 of the Employment Rights Act 1996 allows the Secretary of State to designate certain agreements as Dismissal Procedures Agreements (DPAs). This has the effect of replacing the statutory right to claim unfair dismissal before an employment tribunal under Part 10 of the Employment Rights Act with access to the

procedures of the DPA for employees who are covered by the agreement.

106.   Such an agreement must meet a number of specific criteria. Among these are:

- a joint application is made to the Secretary of State by all parties to the agreement, and

- the scheme offers remedies that are on the whole as beneficial (but not necessarily identical with) those provided in respect of unfair dismissal at an employment tribunal.

107.   This section gives the Secretary of State the power to add to these criteria. This is intended to give scope to bring in requirements aimed at ensuring that DPAs comply with the <u>Human Rights Act 1998</u>.

108.   This is brought about by giving the Secretary of State power by order to add to the requirements in section 110(3) Employment Rights Act 1996.

Section 45: Fixed term work

109.   At the time of publication, fixed term employees are protected by statutory employment rights in the same way as permanent employees, with a few exceptions. However, whereas part-time workers are now protected by legislation preventing them from being less favourably treated than comparable full-time workers, no such provision currently exists in respect of fixed term employees. There are also no restrictions on the use of successive fixed term employment contracts in UK law at the time of publication.

110.   Directive 1999/70/EC concerning the framework agreement on fixed term work was agreed on 28 June 1999 and is due to be implemented in the UK in 2002. The purpose of the framework agreement is to apply the principle of non-discrimination to those in fixed term employment and to establish a framework to prevent abuse arising from the use of successive fixed term employment contracts or relationships. The Government takes the view that, on account of its legal base, this directive does not apply to pay and pensions. However, a public consultation on Fixed Term Work (May 2001) revealed that significant pay disparities exist between fixed term and permanent employees and the Government intends to prevent pay and pensions discrimination against fixed term employees, in addition to implementing directive 1999/70/EC.

111.   This section introduces a power that places a duty on the Secretary of State to make regulations preventing less favourable treatment of fixed term employees and preventing abuse arising from the use of successive periods of fixed term employment.

112.   The section places a duty on the Secretary of State to make regulations in respect of fixed term employees. These regulations will implement directive 1999/70/EC and

prevent pay and pensions discrimination against fixed term employees. A transposition note setting out how the Government will transpose the main elements of this Directive into UK law is available on the DTI website.

113. In particular, these regulations may:

- Prevent less favourable treatment of fixed term employees as compared to permanent employees

- Specify circumstances in which fixed term employment is to have effect as permanent employment

- Specify circumstances in which fixed term contracts are to be taken to be successive

- Specify classes of person taken to be fixed term and permanent employees

- Specify circumstances in which fixed term employees are taken to be, or not to be, treated less favourably than permanent employees

- Amend provisions in specified enactments of primary legislation that allow for some or all fixed term employees to be treated less favourably than permanent employees.

114. The affirmative resolution procedure applies to the making of regulations under this section.

Section 46: Fixed-term work: Northern Ireland

115. This section is similar to section 45 in that it introduces a power requiring the Department for Employment and Learning in Northern Ireland to make regulations preventing less favourable treatment of fixed term employees and preventing abuse arising from the use of successive periods of fixed term employment.

116. The section requires the Department for Employment and Learning to make regulations in respect of fixed term employees. These regulations will implement directive 1999/70/EC and prevent pay and pensions discrimination against those in fixed term employment. In particular, these regulations may:

- Prevent less favourable treatment of fixed term employees as compared to permanent employees

- Specify circumstances in which fixed term employment is to have effect as permanent employment

- Specify circumstances in which fixed term contracts are to be taken to be successive

- Specify classes of person taken to be fixed term and permanent employees

- Specify circumstances in which fixed term employees are taken to be, or not to be, treated less favourably than permanent employees

- Amend provisions in specified enactments of primary legislation that allow for some or all fixed term employees to be treated less favourably than permanent employees.

117. This power is taken at the request of the Minister for Employment and Learning in Northern Ireland, and with the agreement of the Northern Ireland Executive. Although employment law is a transferred matter under the Northern Ireland Act 1998, an enabling section could not be included in a corresponding Northern Ireland Assembly Act, as Fixed Term Work Regulations are required to be made in Northern Ireland by 2002, and this leaves insufficient time for the passage of a Northern Ireland Employment Act with its own enabling section.

Section 47 and Schedule 7: Flexible working

118. Flexible working was the single biggest issue raised by consultees during the consultation for the 'Work and Parents: Competitiveness and Choice' Green Paper of December 2000. Responding to this, in June 2001, the Secretary of State for Trade and Industry set up the independent Work and Parents Taskforce to examine how to meet parents' desire for more flexible work patterns in a way that is compatible with business efficiency. This section therefore gives parents the right to apply for flexible working. It lays out:

- The eligibility criteria which must be met in order for an employee to apply for a flexible working pattern;

- A clearly defined framework for a procedure to be followed by employees and employers when making and considering requests for flexible working;

- The employer's duties in relation to an application under the new provisions;

- The right for an employee to take their case to an employment tribunal; and

- What happens if a tribunal finds that an application has not been dealt with correctly.

119. The new provisions will be inserted into the Employment Rights Act 1996.

80F Statutory right to request contract variation

120.   Section 80F sets out the criteria that must be satisfied in order for an employee to be eligible to make a request for a flexible working pattern. It is intended to ensure that requests are not made on the spur of the moment and as such the employee will have to make a formal application containing specified information.

121.   Subsection (1) identifies the kind of variations of the terms and conditions a qualifying employee may apply to his employer for under this part of the Act. It is intended that the changes are limited to the hours the employee is required to work, the times he is required to work, and where he is required to work. The intention is that this will cover work patterns such as compressed hours; flexitime; home working; job-sharing; teleworking; term-time working; shift working; staggered hours; annualised hours; self-rostering. By regulations, the Secretary of State may also specify further criteria if it is found at a later date that the list is not exhaustive enough to cover all the changes that may be needed.

122.   Subsection (1) also makes clear that these changes can only be made for the purpose of caring for a child. The right to apply will be available to a qualifying employee who has a relationship with the child, which will be specified in regulations. It is intended that this will cover anyone who has responsibility as a parent of an eligible child. For example, biological parents, adoptive parents, and new partners of parents where they share the responsibility of caring for the child. It is not the intention that the ability to apply for flexible working should extend as far as anyone who lives in the same house as the child but does not have responsibility for caring for the child e.g. grandparents, aunts, uncles (unless they specifically have parental responsibility).

123.   Subsection (2) sets out what must be included in an application. Qualifying employees will have to explain why they are eligible for making a request i.e. self-certify. The effect of an application being accepted will result in a variation of the terms and conditions of an employee's contract of employment. This means that should an employer subsequently discover that their employee has lied and never intended to use the flexible working pattern for the purposes of caring for the child then they may take disciplinary action.

124.   Subsection (3) specifies the age limits of the child. The ability to request flexible working will be open to those employees who care for children under six years of age so as to cover two periods when the levels of requests are expected to be high; that is, the time following the child's birth and when the child starts school. Regulations will allow for the possibility of changing the age limit in the light of experience (subsection (6)). Parents of disabled children face greater challenges in raising their children and they will be able to make requests up until their child is 18 years of age. It is not the intention of the Government that it will use this power in the short-term. The Government will first review the right three years after it comes into force.

125.   Subsection (4) deals with the frequency of applications. It limits the number of requests an employee may make to one per year, from the date the application is

made, because of the costs of dealing with an application. The latest an employee will be able to make an application is 14 days before their child reaches either age limit. Once this time period is reached, the employee will no longer have the right to apply to change their working pattern and their existing working pattern will continue. The Work and Parents Taskforce did not find a willingness amongst employers and employees for undoing the original changes made to implementing a flexible working pattern when either of the limits is reached.

126. Subsection (5) provides for regulations allowing changes to how an application should be made.

127. Subsection (7) provides that the reference to a disabled child for the purposes of this section is to a child claiming disability living allowance within the meaning of Section 71 of the Social Security Contributions and Benefits Act 1992.

128. Subsection (8) provides the power to establish the criteria under which a person will be classed as an employee for the purposes of making an application. It is intended that the requirement as to duration of employment will be continuous service with the same employer for at least 26 weeks. Agency workers who are employees will not be eligible to make a request. This is for practical reasons. The agency will not have a detailed knowledge of the business of the company with which the agency worker is placed to be in a position deal with an application. On the other hand the company with which the agency worker is placed will have approached the agency to provide a specific service without an expectation of having to adjust their working patterns to the individual's circumstances.

80G Employers' duties in relation to applications under section 80F

129. Regulations will be made concerning an employer's duties in relation to dealing with applications for flexible working.

130. When an employer receives a request it will be their duty to accept it or to establish the business case for rejecting it and they will need to follow a prescribed procedure to ensure and demonstrate that the request has been properly dealt with. The aim is to encourage dialogue between the employer and employee in the workplace about changing work patterns and how to meet both parties' needs.

131. There will be occasions where an employer believes that they are unable to accept a request. In order to reject an application they must, in their opinion, have specific business grounds for doing so. Subsection (1) (b) specifies what each of these are:

- The burden of additional costs;

- Detrimental effect on ability to meet customer demand;

- Inability to re-organise work among existing staff;

- Inability to recruit additional staff;

- Detrimental impact on quality;

- Detrimental impact on performance;

- Insufficiency of work during the periods the employee proposes to work; and,

- Planned structural changes.

132.	There is a power to make regulations to add to these grounds if the Secretary of State becomes aware of other grounds that should be included. The section contains all those identified by the Taskforce. Employers will not be able to simply tick a box saying one or more grounds exist but will have to provide sufficient explanation to the employee of why, in their opinion, the ground applies to their business and why it results in the refusal of the application.

133.	Subsection (2) identifies regulations that are intended to outline the procedure for dealing with an application for flexible working. In practice, the intended procedure will work as follows:

- A request is received specifying the desired working pattern, the date from which it is proposed it should apply, and explaining what effect the employee thinks the change will have on the employer and how it might be accommodated. The employee will have to explain why they are eligible under the right to make an application.

- The employer arranges a meeting within 28 days of receiving the application to discuss the request. The employee is able to bring a representative if they wish.

- The employer writes to the employee within 14 days of the meeting either (i) agreeing the new working pattern, any action on which it is dependent, and a start date; or (ii) confirming any compromise suggested and the start date; or (iii) setting out the business reasons and an explanation of why the request cannot be met, together with details of how to appeal if the employee is not content with the decision.

- An employee has 14 days following the notification of their employer's decision to appeal.

- Within 14 days of being informed that the employee wishes to appeal the employer should arrange a further meeting to hear the appeal. The employee may be accompanied by a representative if they wish.

- The employer must provide a decision within 14 days of hearing the appeal.

134. The practical details of the procedure for both employees and employers will be specified in regulations. This is to ensure that all the details can be kept together. It is the intention that these will define how the meetings are to be arranged and the arrangements for postponement in circumstances where one of the parties is unable to attend. The regulations will explain who can accompany the employee. It is the intention, as the Taskforce recommended, that this will be a fellow employee, friend or appropriate recognised trade union representative. The Taskforce did not want unduly to limit the people who could accompany the parent making the request and preferred a wider formula that would encompass all expertise in this area. The Government intends to consult widely on this issue. The regulations will also detail the points that will need to be covered when informing the employee of the employer's decision. Where an employer rejects an application the intention is that the employer should set out their business reasons (which will have to be from the list shown above) backed up with an explanation of the reason why, in their opinion, it applies. This is to help the employee understand why the employer has arrived at his decision and to help demonstrate that the request has been considered seriously. It is envisaged that a couple of paragraphs will usually be sufficient. The intention is that the guidance to accompany the right will include a variety of differing examples for each of the business reasons. One illustrative explanation might be:

> "I am sorry that I cannot grant your request to leave at 3:30pm each day as this will severely effect our ability to meet customer demand and I am unable to cover your absence. You are currently the only certified forklift truck driver that works at the end of the day and it is essential that we are able to load the lorries for over-night delivery. Due to the fact that we supply perishable goods it is not possible to load the delivery lorries any earlier in the day. I have spoken with our other two forklift truck drivers, and they are presently unable to change their hours. I also advertised in the local paper when Sam left and notified the Job Centre of the vacancy but could not find anyone to cover his job. As that was only two months ago it is not appropriate to go through the process again now."

135. The regulations will also cover the appeal process. The intention is that the employee will have to set out the grounds for their appeal. These grounds may include, but need not be confined, to the following: concern that the procedure has not been properly followed, that the business reasons for rejecting the request have not been sufficiently explained, or that a fact in the explanation of the business reasons is incorrect. The intention is that the appeal should be held with a more senior manager than the initial meeting where possible. This will not always be possible especially for small businesses. The regulations will also explain the points that the employer should cover when informing the employee of the outcome of the appeal. The intention is that the employer should give a sufficient explanation, building on the earlier communication where appropriate. Where the procedure has been followed correctly (either up until the appeal stage or through the appeal stage itself) then it is the Government's intention that the employee should not be able to claim a grievance

against the employer when informed of the outcome just because they do not like it. It is intended to make use of the regulations elsewhere in the Employment Act to disapply the three-step grievance procedure in these circumstances. It is also the intention that the regulations will allow for the appeal to be heard as part of an employer's established procedure for handling appeals on other issues, as long as the timescales are no less than those for the appeal procedure described above. This is to encourage the employer and employee to use all the avenues open to them to try and find a satisfactory outcome.

136.   Subsection (3) enables regulations under subsection (1)(a) to disapply any part of the procedure if an application is agreed or withdrawn; to provide for an application to be treated as withdrawn in specified circumstances; and to provide for a time limit to be extended, for example if the employer and employee agree the extension.

137.   Regulations will allow for:

- Changes to the procedure where there is agreement between both parties. For example, the employer may feel able to accept the request immediately and thus a meeting would be inappropriate.

- Changes to the timescales where there is agreement between both parties. This is to cover circumstances where it may be extremely difficult for one party to follow a certain part of the procedure. For example it may be that during the meeting to discuss the request an alternative is identified but further information is needed to ensure that it is workable. It may not always be possible in the circumstances for this information to be obtained within the two weeks the employer has to notify the employee of their decision. It is the intention that the regulations will specify how the agreement to postpone is to be handled and recorded.

- The request to be treated as withdrawn in some circumstances. The intention is that where an employee fails repeatedly to attend the meeting and to answer letters without proper explanation then the employer should be able to conclude that the employee no longer wishes to pursue the request to work flexibly.

138.   Subsection (4) allows Subsection (2) to be amended by order. This enables the procedure for making an application to be changed at a later date if it is found necessary to do so.

80H Complaints to employment tribunals

139.   Where cases cannot be resolved in the workplace or through other alternative dispute resolution mechanisms (employees will be able to use the Advisory Conciliation and Arbitration Service binding arbitration scheme), an employee will be able to take their

case to an employment tribunal.

- Subsection (1) identifies the circumstances under which an employee who has made an application under 80F may present a complaint to an employment tribunal.

- Subsection (2) clarifies that no complaint can be presented to an employment tribunal in respect of an application which has been disposed of by agreement or withdrawn.

- Subsection (3) clarifies that in the case of an application that has not been disposed of by agreement or withdrawn, a complaint cannot be made under this section until either the employer notifies the employee of a decision to reject the application on appeal or commits a breach of regulations under section 80G(1)(a).

- Subsection (4) provides that a complaint cannot be made under this section in respect of a failure to comply with regulations under section 80G(2)(k), (l) or (m). This is because the regulations themselves will include a right to complain to the employment tribunal in such cases.

- Subsections (5) and (6) explain that a complaint cannot be presented to an employment tribunal unless it is made within three months of the date on which the employee is notified of the employers' decision on the appeal, or of the breach of the regulations, unless there is an extension under subsection (3)(b). However, it allows for the cases to be heard after this time limit if the tribunal feels it was not reasonably practicable for the complaint to be made within it.

80I Remedies

140. This new section outlines what will happen if an employment tribunal finds a complaint under section 80H well founded.

- Subsection (1) provides that if a tribunal finds that a complaint is well founded, the tribunal will have the power to order an employer to reconsider a request. It also gives a tribunal the power to consider whether an award of compensation should be made to the employee in such circumstances.

- Subsection (2) enables the tribunal to make the award of compensation at a level they feel to be just and equitable given the specific circumstances of the case. In deciding the amount, the tribunal will take into account the behaviour of the employer (e.g. whether they have lied) and of the employee (e.g. their willingness to consider acceptable alternatives).

- Subsection (3), however, limits any compensation award to a maximum to be specified in regulations. There will be consultation on regulations to specify how many weeks pay should be the maximum.

141. Schedule 7 provides for amendments to other legislation which are consequential on the amendments made by section 47. These include an amendment to the Trade Union and Labour Relations Act (Consolidation) 1992 to allow disputes over flexible working to be settled under the ACAS arbitration scheme and to the Employment Rights Act 1996 to exclude the Armed Forces from these provisions.

Section 48: Rate of maternity allowance

142. This section amends section 35A of the Social Security Contributions and Benefits Act 1992, which sets out the weekly rate of MA by replacing subsections (1) to (3) of section 35(A):

- Subsection (1)(a) inserts a new subsection (1) so that women eligible for MA will be paid the lesser of 90% of their average weekly earnings or the prescribed standard rate, for the duration of the payment period.

- Subsection (1)(b) amends the current subsection (5)(c)(i) to ensure that women who have paid a Class 2 contribution are deemed to have earnings at a level 90% of which will equal the flat rate of SMP, for any week within the specified period. As a result, they will be entitled to £100 per week. This, together with subsection (1)(c) ensures that (as now) a self-employed woman who has paid a Class 2 contribution throughout the specified period will receive standard rate MA.

- Subsection (2) is a transitional provision ensuring that reference may be made to current rates where appropriate after the coming into force of the maternity pay provisions contained in this Act.

Section 49: Work-focused interviews for partners

143. Partners of working age benefit claimants who are themselves of working age will be required to take part in a work-focused interview, in default of which, benefit sanctions will apply. This will provide partners with the opportunity to discuss their skills and experience, the barriers they face in moving closer to the labour market and the help and support that is available to overcome those barriers. The measure will not place any requirement on partners beyond taking part in interviews. (For example, they will not be required to attend training courses or seek work).

Section 2AA: Full entitlement to certain benefits conditional on work-focused interview for partner

144. This section builds on section 2A of the Social Security Administration Act 1992 ("the Administration Act"), which was inserted by section 57 of the Welfare Reform

and Pensions Act 1999 and which introduced the requirement for certain benefit claimants (including lone parents) to attend work-focused interviews. The new section 2AA prescribes both the circumstances in which the partner of a benefit claimant may be required to take part a work-focused interview, and the consequences for the benefit claim if the partner does not take part in the interview.

145. The work-focused interview will concentrate on job potential and provide the partner with access to a wide range of help and information on work, benefits and services such as childcare. It is intended to encourage partners to take further steps towards labour market participation. However, any action they may choose to take beyond taking part in the interviews will be entirely voluntary.

146. This section inserts new section 2AA into the Administration Act and allows the Secretary of State to prescribe in regulations that where a higher rate of a specified benefit is payable to a person by reference to his partner, then the claimant's benefit can be reduced by way of a sanction if the partner fails to take part in a work-focused interview, when required to do so.

147. The intention is for the actual proposals to be prescribed in secondary legislation to allow adjustments to be made to the detailed aspects of the scheme in the light of experience of work-focused interviews.

148. The power itself:

   - Subsection (1) allows the Secretary of State to make regulations requiring partners of claimants for certain benefits to take part in a work-focused interview, in prescribed circumstances. Once the claimant's entitlement to benefit has been established their partner may be required to take part in a work-focused interview. If partners do not take part in these interviews without good cause when required to do so, a benefit sanction will apply (see *subsection* (4)(f). As the majority of jobseekers find work within the first six months of a claim it is initially intended that partners will be required to attend an interview at the 6 month stage of a claim, thus focusing resources on those partners who need more help in finding work. The timing of interviews will be considered further in the light of experience of work-focused interviews for benefit claimants.

   - Subsection (2) lists the benefits to which the partner work-focused interview requirements will apply. Subsection (3) lists the circumstances in which a higher rate of such a benefit is deemed to be payable to a person by reference to his partner and therefore, the partner is subject to the requirement to take part in an interview.

149. How the power is intended to be used:

   - Subsections (4) to (6) identify the main ways in which the regulation-making powers provided under subsection (1) might be used. Where a person is entitled to a number of specified benefits at the same time, it is not intended to ask their partner to take part in separate work-focused interviews for each benefit. They would only be required to take part in one interview. Subsection (4)(a) allows for regulations to achieve this.

- Subsection (4)(b) allows for regulations to prescribe that where a claimant is entitled to benefit for more than one partner (i.e. in the case of a polygamous marriage) each of those partners will be required to take part in a work-focused interview.

- Subsection (4)(c) enables the Secretary of State to prescribe in regulations who will conduct the interviews with partners. This means that work-focused interviews may be conducted by a person acting on behalf of the Secretary of State, by a local authority employee, or by a private/voluntary sector organisation contracted to provide services.

- Regulations under subsection (4)(d) will confer power on those who conduct the interviews with partners to determine where and when an interview will take place. This mirrors section 8 of the Jobseekers Act 1995 and section 2A of the Administration Act. It is intended that the interview will usually be conducted at a range of easily accessible premises. However, where partners cannot reasonably be expected to visit an office, a more suitable location including a home visit may be arranged.

- Subsection (4)(e) enables regulations to prescribe the circumstances in which partners are to be treated as either taking part or not taking part in the interview. Since the regulations under this section will impose a general requirement on partners to take part in a work-focused interview, both the partners and those who conduct the interviews need to be clear about the criteria to be used in judging whether a person has actually taken part in the interview. It is intended that the test of whether partners have taken part will be: (a) whether they attend at the time and place specified; and (b) whether they provide information in areas relevant to their employment prospects, such as their level of educational qualifications, their previous work history, and any barriers to work they may face.

- Subsection (4)(f) enables regulations to provide that if a partner is requested to take part in an interview but does not do so then, unless he (or the benefit claimant) can show good cause for that failure within a prescribed period, the claimant's benefit will be reduced.

- Subsection (4)(g) enables regulations to specify what constitutes good cause for not taking part in an interview. *Good cause* is a familiar concept in social security. For example, it is used in relation to work-focused interviews for claimants under section 2A of the Administration Act and in deciding whether people's entitlement to Jobseeker's Allowance should stop where they have not attended as required as a specified time and place (section 8(1)(d) of the Jobseekers Act 1995 and regulations 28 to 30 of the Jobseeker's Allowance Regulations 1996). Examples of good cause might be when the partner had an accident on the day set for the interview or where their child fell ill or where they misunderstood the requirements placed upon them because of any language or literacy difficulties.

- Subsection (5) deals with how any reduction in benefit should be calculated and applied.

- Subsection (5)(a) enables regulations to specify how the reduction will normally be calculated and subsection (5)(b) enables regulations to specify that the amount of the reduction shall be restricted in prescribed circumstances. The power under subsection (5)(b) will be used where the amount of the reduction would otherwise be greater than the amount of benefit. In addition, it is the intention to ensure that the claimant retains entitlement to a nominal amount, to prevent the claim from lapsing and, where appropriate, to ensure that entitlement to any "passported" benefits (such as free NHS Prescriptions, free school meals) is retained.

- Subsection (5)(c) enables regulations to specify that if a person is claiming more than one benefit, the sanction may be applied to more than one of the benefits; but the total sanction must not exceed the amount calculated in regulations under subsection (5)(a). The regulations will also prioritise the benefits against which the sanction is to be applied. No sanctions will be applied against any benefit not specified in new section 2AA(2).

- Subsection (6) enables regulations to prescribe the circumstances in which the requirement for a partner to take part in a work-focused interview is not to be applied. This is so that the interview can be waived or deferred until a later date if that is necessary or appropriate in any case. There will be certain people for whom a work-focused interview will not be appropriate. There is no intention to set out in regulations the categories of people for whom this would be appropriate. Such decisions will be made on a case-by-case basis, depending on the circumstances of the individual.

- Subsection (6)(a) enables regulations to specify circumstances in which the requirement to take part in a work-focused interview will not apply to a partner: either permanently or until a specified time. It is intended that this power will be used to exempt partners of people who are claiming the benefits listed in subsection (2) but who are required to attend work-focused interviews in their own right.

- Subsection (6)(b) enables the 'designated authority' to decide that the requirement to take part in a work-focused interview is not to apply where it would not be of assistance or appropriate in the particular circumstances of that person. Regulations will not specify which groups should have the requirement waived although one example might be where a terminally ill person is the partner of a benefit claimant.

- Subsection (6)(c) enables the 'designated authority' to decide that the requirement to take part in a work-focused interview should be deferred if it is determined that an interview would not be of assistance, or appropriate, at that particular time. Examples might include a person in the early stages of recovery from a major operation, or a partner who had just given birth. Regulations provided for under subsection (6) may also set out that, where a partner has their interview waived or deferred, they will be treated, as having met the requirement – until such time as it is appropriate for them to attend an interview. Where an interview is either waived or deferred (see subsection (6)(c)), despite the fact that there has been no interview, no change will be made to the amount of benefit payable or in payment.

- Subsection (7) defines terms used throughout the section. A "*work-focused interview*" is the interview that almost all partners of claimants of the benefits listed in subsection (2) will be asked to take part in. The purpose of such an interview is to assist or encourage partners to improve their employment prospects over time, and to identify and take steps to overcome the barriers to work they face through training or specialist support so that, where appropriate, they can move towards education or taking up employment (whether paid or unpaid). To this end, an interview may cover such areas as previous employment record, capacity to undertake work, the in-work financial support which is available and help in areas such as childcare, housing and training.

150. Schedule 7 (Paragraphs 8 to 10, 14 and 49): makes minor and consequential amendments to the Administration Act and to the Social Security Act 1998.

- Paragraph 9 amends section 2B of the Administration Act, which makes further provision as to how the power in section 2A may be used. It ensures that the decisions and appeals procedures in Chapter II of Part I of the Social Security Act 1998 apply in relation to any "relevant decisions" under the new section 2AA. It also provides that any decision that a partner has, without good cause, failed to take part in an interview as required by the new section 2AA may be revised or appealed against. It also sets out in that section what are to be "relevant decisions" under the new section 2AA – namely, decisions that someone has failed, without good cause, to take part in an interview required under that section, and makes a consequential amendment in relation to decisions under section 2A. It ensures that all "relevant decisions" under the new section 2AA are treated as having been made by the Secretary of State – even if the decision maker is not a civil servant, and that such a decision may be revised or superseded by someone other than the original decision maker.

The powers in the Social Security Act 1998 to revise or supersede a decision would then apply. It would also allow for information gathered about a person's employability to be passed on to the relevant decision maker.

- Paragraph 10 amends section 2C of the Administration Act so as to ensure that the powers, which are intended to enable closer working between central and local government in order to make the delivery of social security benefits more customer-focused and better co-ordinated, also apply to the new section 2AA.

- Paragraph 14 amends section 190(1) of the Administration Act so as to require the first set of regulations to be made under the new section 2AA to be passed by the affirmative resolution procedure.

- Paragraph 49 amends the Social Security Act 1998 so as to provide that the right of appeal is against the decision that the partner had failed to take part in an interview, rather than the decision to stop or reduce benefit. It focuses on the one decision that causes a penalty to be imposed (which may potentially be across a number of benefits) and is intended to avoid confusion.

Section 50: Use of information for, or relating to, employment and training

151. This section introduces schedule 6.

152. Government policies in the area of employment and social security have focused on increasing the efforts to help people move away from welfare benefits and into work. However, once a client has left an employment or training programme or has come off benefit, they are under no obligation to inform the Department for Work and Pensions (DWP) of their activities. It is important that DWP know what happens to people afterwards. Many clients do provide DWP with this information. However, a significant minority do not. Attempts to establish the destinations of leavers are costly, time consuming and inconclusive. In addition, once a client has entered work, DWP has no way of assessing their progress in employment, unless they return to benefit. This creates two problems. The first is in evaluating the effectiveness of employment and training initiatives in moving people into sustainable work. The second is in paying and rewarding providers, who are increasingly paid on a performance-related basis. The provisions will also allow DWP to confirm which clients have moved into work and ensure the security of the funding arrangements.

153. Commentary on Schedule 6:

- Paragraph 1 amends section 3 of the Social Security Act 1998 by broadening the range of information covered by the Act, which already covered social security, child support, and war pensions, to also include employment and training. This means that the Secretary of State or the Northern Ireland Department can use the information held by him for the purpose of, or any purpose connected with the exercise of any of those functions. This therefore allows DWP to use any of the information it holds to perform any of its functions. Following the transfer of war pensions to the Ministry of Defence (MOD), the provision will also enable the supply of information to and from MOD and DWP to enable the supply of social security, child support and employment and training information to MOD for use for war pensions purposes and the supply of war pensions information from MOD to DWP for social security, child support or employment and training purposes. The provision also allows the data pooling of information relating to any of these functions, ie. social security, child support, war pensions and employment and training.

- Paragraph 4 repeals subsection (3) of that section as that is now rendered otiose by the amendments made by paragraphs 2 and 3.

- Paragraphs 2 and 3 amend the existing provisions in sections 122C and 122D which govern the supply of information to and from DWP, the Northern Ireland Department and local authorities in connection with the administration of housing and council tax benefit. These sections are extended to include employment and training information.

- Paragraph 5 amends section 122 of the Administration Act to allow DWP access to tax information held by IR and information held by Customs and Excise for the purposes of preventing fraud against the DWP by those contracted to deliver employment and training programmes and possible fraud by participants in the schemes. The amendment will also enable errors to be checked where no fraud is suspected. Paragraph 7 makes corresponding provision for Northern Ireland.

- Paragraph 6 inserts a new section 122ZA into the Administration Act allowing DWP to access PAYE information held by Revenue as well as information supplied by the self-employed for tax purposes relating to people beginning or terminating employment. The information can be used for the purposes of evaluating the effectiveness of various employment and training programmes (such as the New Deals). This gives DWP access to the information supplied by employers on tax forms P45 and P46, which will allow the Department to ascertain whether leavers from employment or training programmes have taken up employment. The subsection states that such information must not be further disclosed, other than for civil or criminal proceedings. Because such information is based upon employers' annual returns, this information will typically be over 18 months old by the time it reaches DWP. Allowing DWP access to the information on P45 and P46 forms will therefore provide them with more up-to-date information. These forms are completed when an employee starts a new job. The only information that will be supplied from this source will be the fact that the individual has started work and the name and address of his employer. The section will apply to all relevant information held when the provision comes into force as well as relevant information gathered after that date.

- Paragraph 8 makes corresponding provision for Northern Ireland.

- Paragraphs 9 and 10 amend the Tax Credits Act 1999 so as to ensure that information to which the DWP has access relating to tax credits can if necessary be used for employment and training purposes and that employment and training information can be supplied to the Revenue for tax credits purposes.

- Paragraph 11 amends section 121E of the Social Security Administration Act 1992 (the "Administration Act"). This section deals with the supply of contributions, statutory sick pay (SSP) and statutory maternity pay (SMP) and contracting out information held by Inland Revenue. The amendment extends the purposes to which information supplied by the Inland Revenue to the DWP can be put, to include purposes relating to employment or training. It specifies that information supplied relating to employment and training may be supplied on a permissive basis – i.e. that the DWP cannot demand information from IR. This amendment will enable information supplied to the DWP by Inland Revenue under provisions in the Administration Act to be used for employment and training purposes. This will provide inter alia information on where the individual is employed, how long they have worked for that employer and how much they earn, all of which is helpful in assessing the effectiveness of the various welfare to work initiatives.

- Paragraph 12 makes corresponding provision for Northern Ireland.

- Paragraph 13 makes similar provision with respect to section 121F of the Administration Act. This section deals with the supply of information to the Inland Revenue by DWP (in the person of the Secretary of State) for the purposes of contributions, SMP and SSP and contracting out. Paragraph 14 makes corresponding provision for Northern Ireland.

SCHEDULES

154. Where necessary, the Schedules are described at relevant points of the main commentary. The table below shows where each Schedule (or Part of a Schedule) is explained.

Schedule	Subject	Refer to commentary on:
1	Penalties: procedures and appeals	

2		Statutory Dispute Resolution Procedures	Section 29
	Part 1	Dismissal and disciplinary procedures	
	Part 2	Grievance procedures	
	Part 3	General Requirements.	
3		Tribunal jurisdictions to which section 31 applies	Section 31
4		Tribunal jurisdictions to which section 33 applies.	Section 33
5		Tribunal jurisdictions to which section 38 applies	Section 38
6		Use of information for, or relating to, employment and training	Section 50
7		Minor and consequential amendments	Section 47 and 48
8		Repeals and revocations	

FINANCIAL EFFECTS OF THE ACT

155.   **Overview** - The predicted impact of the provisions relating to each individual policy is dealt with separately below in terms of costs to the Exchequer:

156.   **Paid paternity leave** – the costs to the Exchequer are estimated to be £63 million in the financial year 2003/4.

157.   **Paid adoption leave** – the costs to the Exchequer are estimated to be £9 million in the financial year 2003/4

158.   **Increase in rate of statutory maternity pay and maternity allowance -** the costs to the Exchequer are estimated to be £355 million in the financial year 2003/4. This cost assumes that 85% of eligible women take advantage of the extended period. Around 305,000 pregnant women receive SMP each year and around 51,000 receive MA each year. It is estimated that around 90% of SMP recipients will benefit in full from the new measures so that each woman in comparison with the level of SMP currently paid will be entitled to £1253.60 more in SMP payments.

159.   **Introduction of partner work-focused interviews -** Initial estimates indicate that the costs to the Exchequer are likely to be around £35 million. The impact on benefit expenditure of increased numbers of partners of benefit claimants taking up work cannot be estimated at this stage. Such behavioural changes cannot be predicted with any certainty until the new system has been operated and evaluated.

160.   **Power to make wasted costs awards** – it is estimated that this will lead to a reduction in caseload, leading to savings for the Exchequer of a little under £1 million.

161.   **Removing procedural traps** – it is estimated that this change will lead to net costs to

the Exchequer of £2 and £5 million.

162. **Fixed period of conciliation** – the savings to the Exchequer of introducing fixed periods of conciliation are estimated at between £2 and £3 million.

163. **Three steps procedures (including mitigation of awards and removal of the small business exemption on written particulars**) - savings for the Exchequer are estimated to be negligible in year one as the system settles in but growing to between £11 and £15 million from year two onwards.

164. **Equal Pay questionnaire** - the savings to the Exchequer in terms of reductions in tribunal cases is estimated at £0.1 million.

165. Measures with no significant financial effects

The following measures in the Act are not expected to have any significant financial effect. Minor increases in operational expenditure, for example as a result of changes required to forms and process will be managed within existing allocations.

- Use of employment and training information

- Union learning representatives

PUBLIC SERVICE STAFFING EFFECTS

166. The only measure in the Act expected to have a significant effect on public service staffing is work-focused interviews for partners. We estimate that up to 650 staff will be needed to deliver the work-focused interviews.

167. **Introduction of partner work-focused interviews -** Initial broad-brush estimates indicate that the costs to the Exchequer are likely to be around £35 million. The impact on benefit expenditure of increased numbers of partners of benefit claimants taking up work cannot be estimated at this stage. Such behavioural changes cannot be predicted with any certainty until the new system has been operated and evaluated.

168. In the longer term there are also likely to be effects from the projected reduction in volumes of applications to employment tribunals.

SUMMARY OF REGULATORY IMPACT ASSESSMENT

Overview of the impact of the Act

169. The overall intention of the Act is to support the development of more productive workplaces in the UK by encouraging participation in the labour market through the

retention and development of skills, and by improving the way that disputes are managed, both at work and within the employment tribunals system. This impact assessment considers the individual proposals and their overall effect. Where they overlap or enhance each other this will be addressed. Self-standing impact assessments are attached for each element of the Act expected to affect business.

170.   All the provisions in the Act will have some impact on the productivity and competitiveness of UK employers, and on the workforce as a whole. Those parts of the Act which relate to dispute resolution are intended to bring benefits, both quantifiable and unquantifiable, to employers and employees through encouraging in-house resolution of disputes without recourse to Employment Tribunals. Unresolved conflict in the workplace can damage morale, increase stress, and may lead to employees quitting their jobs. Equally, disputes taken to Employment Tribunals reduce productivity because of the resources taken up in the legal process and because of their effects on the morale and motivation both of the individuals directly affected, and in the workplace more generally.

171.   The parts of the Act dealing with maternity, paternity and adoption pay and leave are intended to encourage greater participation in the labour market, and the retention of skills, for parents who might otherwise leave the labour market. In addition, there are motivational and productivity benefits through relieving the stress and strain felt by new parents. The provisions in the Act which place union learning representatives on a statutory footing will also enhance productivity by encouraging workforce development. The proposal to extend the European Directive on fixed term work to include pay and pensions will ensure that fixed term contract employees are not discriminated against and will thereby increase employee security and remove a potential distortion in the labour market. The provisions that introduce work-focused interviews for partners of people receiving working-age benefits will also have a positive impact on participation in the labour market but are not included in the Impact Assessment as they do not impose any cost or burden on business.

172.   Quantified costs and benefits are expressed in current (2000/01) prices with the exception of the provisions for maternity pay, paternity leave and pay and adoption leave and pay. For consistency with public expenditure plans, these are expressed in 2003/04 prices.

Better dispute management

173.   The Act provides for improved dispute resolution in the workplace and in the employment tribunal system. Existing problems in the current system of dispute resolution have contributed towards increasing numbers of Employment Tribunal applications. These are putting employers, employees and the tribunal system itself under strain. A dispute resolved in the workplace, especially one resolved early and informally, will reduce workplace tensions and increase retention of valuable staff. A dispute resolved in a Tribunal often leads to the end of the employment relationship. For the employee this means the loss of a job; for the employer it means unnecessary

recruitment and lost skills. And where a dispute does have to go through the Tribunal process, cases should be resolved more quickly, reducing uncertainty for applicants and employers alike.

174. The Act contains several measures to address this. Not all of them have implications that need to be assessed in a regulatory impact assessment. Those included in the RIA are:

- Implied term of contract to confer right/obligation to follow 'three steps' grievance and discipline procedures;

- All written statements of terms and conditions to include reference to workplace procedures (removal of small firms exemption);

- Tribunals to mitigate awards to reflect whether three steps were followed and whether terms and conditions were provided;

- Removing procedural traps in unfair dismissal cases;

- Fixed period of conciliation in all Tribunal cases;

- Changes to reduce wasted costs;

- Introduction of questionnaires in equal pay cases.

175. The individual paragraphs below contain costs and benefit estimates for these provisions. There are strong overlaps between most of these proposals. The total benefits and costs are less than the sum of the individual benefits and costs.

176. Proposals for (i) Implied term of contract to confer right/obligation to follow 'three steps' grievance and discipline procedures; (ii) All written statements of terms and conditions to include reference to workplace procedures (removal of small firms exemption); and (iii) Tribunals to mitigate awards to reflect whether three steps were followed and whether terms and conditions were provided

177. All employers will have to introduce a satisfactory (that is, according to minimum standards) 3-step dispute and grievance procedure to deal with employment issues arising in the workplace. Employees are also obliged to use this procedure. If either party does not fulfil their obligation, this will be reflected in the award.

178. This provides both employees and employers with an incentive to start a discussion about any problems, which may arise. This should in the medium to longer term improve employment relationships and open up the way both parties handle conflicts. Employers will feel the benefit of a clear transparent process that helps them to resolve problems. Employees who otherwise would have left because they felt they had been treated unfairly, or because the relationship had deteriorated over the

months leading up to a Tribunal case, may now decide to stay.

179.   The evidence suggests that most large employers have procedures that already meet the minimum standard. A disproportionate share of tribunal applications arise in workplaces where procedures are absent or have not been followed adequately. Greater use of procedures should therefore reduce significantly the volume of tribunal applications.

180.   The estimated reduction in the number of applications is between 30,000 and 40,000 applications per year. Employers save time and money (£60– 80 million), employees save their own time and reduce stress levels and there are savings to the taxpayer through fewer cases (£11–15 million). There will be a time lag between the more widespread introduction of procedures in firms and a reduction in Tribunal applications of perhaps one year.

181.   There are costs to employers. There are one-off costs arising from the introduction or revision of disciplinary and grievance procedures where these do not already meet the minimum requirements, and from incorporating these into the written statement of employment (£46–86 million). There are also on-going costs arising from the management time involved in greater use of these procedures (£42–90 million per year).

Removing procedural traps in unfair dismissal cases

182.   Some employers have lost faith in the Tribunal system because they believe they will lose an unfair dismissal case because of a small procedural mistake, even if following the correct procedure would have made no difference to the outcome. The new policy is that, in cases where it can be shown that the mistake would not have made a difference to whether a dismissal was fair or unfair, the Tribunal will have the opportunity of disregarding the procedural error. This will only apply for procedures that go over and above the 3-step procedures that will now be part of the contract of employment.

183.   This change should discourage some Tribunal applications based mainly on procedural error. The benefits to employers are £6-11 million per year. Of these about £4-6 million are transfers from employees due to changes in the structure of tribunal outcomes. The benefits to the taxpayer are about £1 million.

184.   The costs of the proposal are also related to the shift in outcomes. Individuals have reduced awards and settlement payments of about £4-6 million. Respondents lose £1-4 million. There are costs to the taxpayer of £2-5 million.

Fixed period of conciliation in all Tribunal cases

185.   A large number of applications are settled with the help of ACAS conciliations (38%). This proportion differs between jurisdictions. In addition, withdrawn cases are

sometimes influenced by ACAS conciliators. Some of the settlements or withdrawals occur just before the hearing. This can be costly for the taxpayer.

186. The provision to be introduced is to use a fixed period for conciliation during which the minds of both parties can focus on the conciliation process.

187. A fixed conciliation period of six weeks aims to increase the number of settlements and reduce the number settling close to a hearing date. The latter effect, in particular, will help the ETS to handle other applications more efficiently.

188. The number of hearings is expected to fall by between 1,700 and 3,400 each year. There are some transfers between respondents and applicants due to a change in the structure of outcomes. There are financial benefits to employers of £3-7 million and to the taxpayer of £2-3 million. Individuals also benefit by £1-2 million from more settled cases at the expense of employers.

Wasted costs

189. The Act includes provisions that provide stronger disincentives to unreasonable behaviour both up to and during the hearing process, through changes to the rules on award of costs and a new provision for awards in respect of a party's preparation time. The tribunal will be able to make an award in respect of time spent by parties in preparing the case where cases or defences are misconceived (which includes having no reasonable prospect of success), or where the other party has behaved unreasonably. Costs awards will be possible against representatives who are acting on a for profit basis where it is their behaviour that has triggered the cost award.

190. The proposals should discourage a small number of weak Tribunal applications (100-500 per year) and will also encourage more settlements and fewer hearings. In addition, more cost awards will be made, providing more compensation to those at the receiving end of unreasonable behaviour.

191. It is estimated that savings to the taxpayer will amount to a little under £1 million per year, together with benefits to employers from less applications of £0.2-1 million. There will also be increased flows of payment between employers and applicants arising from the increased use of cost awards. Applicants are expected to benefit by £0.4-0.5 million whereas respondents are expected to benefit by £0.7-1.1 million (respondents benefit more because they are likely to incur more management time and legal representation in dealing with a Tribunal application).

Equal Pay questionnaire

192. The Act introduces a formal questionnaire procedure for use in equal pay tribunal cases, with time limits for an employer response. The purpose of the procedure is to help the potential applicant decide whether to institute proceedings and to help them to formulate and present their case. This enables the key facts to be settled quickly

and can encourage not only the swift establishment of evidence but also the settlement of cases.

193.   Introduction of the questionnaire procedure is expected to lead to a 10% reduction in the number of equal pay Tribunal applications. Benefits to the taxpayer are estimated to be £0.1 million. Employer benefits are estimated at £0.5 million.

194.   Total costs to employers of completing the questionnaire procedure are estimated to be between £ 0.2 and £ 0.4 million.

Overall effect of dispute resolution procedures

195.   The overall effect of the proposals above is not the sum of each individual proposal. Several proposals address the same or closely related issues. Their effects therefore overlap.

196.   The tables on pages 46 and 47, on the overarching effects of the dispute resolution proposals, set out the assumptions made in calculating the overall impact of these proposals.

197.   The most significant proposal in terms of impact is the introduction of grievance and disciplinary procedures as a contractual right. If this is implemented, fewer disputes will go to Tribunals - thus reducing the costs and benefits of almost all of the above proposals that address cases that do reach Tribunals.

198.   The total effect of the proposals is estimated to be a reduction in the number of applications of 23-31% or by between 30,000 and 40,000 applications (using current application volumes as a starting point)[3]. The related benefits to employers are estimated to be £65-91 million once the proposals have fed through into reduced Tribunal applications. The taxpayer will benefit by £13-18 million and individuals by £1-2 million. There are some costs to employers especially due to the introduction of procedures. One off costs are £46-86 million. The use of procedures leads to ongoing costs of £42-90 million. Employers who already have and use procedures will not face additional costs. The other proposals add a further £2-4 million. Costs to the taxpayer are mostly related to changes in the outcome of applications and are therefore policy costs not implementation costs. These are £1-3 million.

Participation in the labour market and retention, and development of skills

Paternity leave and pay

_____

[3] ETS has only been able to deal with 70% of application in 2000/01. The benefits to ETS are therefore built on 70% of the estimated reduction in the number of cases.

199.   The law will provide fathers with an entitlement of 2 weeks paid leave (at £100 per week) to be taken during the first 8 weeks of the child's life. The intended effect is to give fathers a chance to support the mother during this crucial period and to assist them in building a relationship with the new child.

200.   The main benefits arise for fathers and their families. In total they will receive £63 million in form of the statutory payments. They also have more time off during a crucial period in their family life.

201.   There are costs for business. Many firms already offer some form of paternity leave, either paid or unpaid. The additional burdens on business are therefore expected to be small. Costs arise from the provision of coverage for absent fathers of £25-42 million. These are recurring costs. Introducing the system costs business about £10 million (one-off) and running the system costs £21-32 million (recurring costs). There are costs to the Government because of the payments made to fathers of £63 million.

Adoption leave and pay

202.   At present, adoptive parents only have the right to unpaid parental leave. It is proposed to give one adoptive parent the statutory right to 26 weeks paid leave at £100 per week or 90% of their average earnings (whichever is lower) and an additional 26 unpaid leave. This will enable adoptive parents to spend one year with the child and establish their new relationship. These changes are expected to come into force in April 2003.

203.   The beneficiaries will be adoptive parents and their children. It is estimated that there will be around 3,550 adoptions per year. They will benefit by a total of £10 million per year due to the payments. This represents a cost to the taxpayer.

204.   Costs to business are to cover for the absent parent. These costs are estimated at £2-3 million per year. Business also has to introduce the necessary payment system. This will be similar to the system for maternity leave. Additional costs will be no more than £1 million.

Maternity Pay

205.   The Act makes changes to Statutory Maternity Pay and Maternity Allowance. The rate of flat-rate weekly payment will increase to the lesser of £100 a week or 90% of the woman's average weekly earnings, and the maximum payment period will increase from 18 weeks to 26 weeks. The notice that a woman must normally give her employer before taking maternity leave will increase from 21 to 28 days.

206.   The aim of these measures is to make it easier for women to achieve a better balance between paid work and family life. It does this in combination with changes to

maternity leave that are being introduced through secondary legislation[4]. The changes will also help women to spend more time with a new- born child. As a result, more mothers may be able to return to employment after maternity leave, retaining skills in the labour market and reducing recruitment costs for employers.

207.   There are direct benefits to mothers in the form of the payments made to them of £325 million per year. The benefits for an individual mother will depend on her personal circumstances. The benefit of £100 is above the earnings threshold for National Insurance Contribution. Recipients will therefore have to pay NI contributions. This benefits the National Insurance Fund by £5 million, whereby each individual mothers pays £1.35 per week.

208.   The Government meets £305 million of the payments to mothers. The £20 million difference between this and the £325 million figure is made up of costs to larger employers who are only able to reclaim 92% of the payments to mothers. Some employers, especially larger ones, will have to change their payroll systems. The costs of this change are unlikely to be significant because many employers use standard software packages that are updated routinely in any case.

Duty to consider requests for flexible working from the parents of young children

209.   The impact of the duty to consider requests for flexible working will depend on how many parents exercise the right and how employers respond. A central estimate of take-up suggests that there could be over 500,000 additional requests each year for flexible working and that about 80% of these will be accepted or a compromise reached. This means that hundreds of thousands of working parents and their families benefit from an improved family life. The economy also benefits – savings in recruitment costs alone are valued at £113 million. However, processing requests and accommodating them is not costless. One-off implementation costs are estimated to be £38 million with annual recurring costs of £286 million.

Putting Union learning representatives (ULR) on a statutory footing

210.   The objective of this provision is to improve the skills of the workforce by increasing the number of ULRs and improving their effectiveness. The provision will further reduce the current uncertainty regarding the position of the ULRs and the time and resources they may use to fulfil their task.

211.   There are benefits to employers and employees. Employers gain from enhanced workforce skills leading to improved productivity, complementary effects between ULRs and the human resources team, increased confidence in staff and improved

---

[4] Cross-reference to government response on maternity pay and leave, paternity and adoption pay and leave.

employment relations and a sense of partnership in the workplace. As far as these benefits are quantifiable, they are estimated to be between £16-33 million, steadily rising with increased effectiveness to between £70-140 million in the eighth year after introduction of this provision.

212. There are some costs to employers which are due to the time spent on training ULRs, the time the ULRs spend in fulfilling their task and the administrative costs of understanding the legislation, handling notices and requests for time off. The increased use of ULRs will increase the first two items of this list. Total costs increase from £7 million in the first year to £26 million in the eighth year after the introduction of the provision.

Preventing pay and pensions discrimination against fixed term employees

213. The Act includes a power to prevent pay and pensions discrimination against fixed-term employees that will be implemented alongside the European directive on fixed term work.

214. There are 1.1-1.3 million FTC employees who are potentially affected by these provisions. A relatively small proportion (28-41,000) will benefit from higher pay with total benefits of £21-30 million per year. Similarly, 55-82,000 FTC employees will benefit from greater occupational provision with total benefits of £33-98 million per year.

215. Costs to employers mirror benefits to employees. The costs of the pay provisions are estimated to be £28-39 million (the difference between costs and benefits is accounted for by employer National Insurance Contributions). The costs of the pension provisions are £33-97 million.

Impact on small businesses

216. The measures proposed in the Act affect businesses of all sizes. The consultation exercises carried out for most of the proposals received responses from small and large businesses. In the main areas - the provisions on dispute resolution and on maternity, paternity and adoption pay and leave - focus groups were convened with small firms. The Small Business Service has been consulted on each of the stand-alone RIAs.

217. The proposal to require minimum disciplinary and grievance procedures is likely to disproportionately affect small firms. This is because they are less likely to have procedures that meet this standard or follow them if they are in place. Hence the costs of introducing them will bear most on small businesses - but so will the benefits through reductions in cases going to Employment Tribunals. The proposal to remove procedural traps may benefit small businesses especially as there is evidence that small firms are most likely to make procedural errors.

218.   There is some evidence to suggest that small firms can find it more difficult than larger businesses to cover for absences because they have a smaller number of people to whom work can be re-allocated.   Hence the costs of covering for absences - especially paternity leave - may be more acute in small firms.

219.   Small firms are less likely to employ FTC employees than larger firms.

Summary Table

Quantifiable Benefits

220.   All amounts in £m, rounded to nearest million except where amounts are less than £1m

	To employers	To individuals	To the taxpayer
Dispute resolution	65–91 (from year 2)	1-2	13-18(from year 2)
Paternity leave and pay		63	
Adoption leave	2	10	
Maternity pay		325	
Duty to consider requests for flexible working	113		
Union learning reps	16–33 (year 1) 70-140 (year 8)		
Fixed term work		54-127	

Quantifiable Costs

221.   All amounts in £m, rounded to nearest million except where amounts are less than £1m

	To employers	To individuals	To the taxpayer
Dispute resolution	46–86 (one-off) 44-94 (recurring)	3–5	1–3
Paternity leave and pay	10 (one-off) 39-64 (recurring)		63 (recurring, transfer)
Adoption leave and pay	1 (one-off) 2-3 (recurring)		9 (recurring, transfer)
Maternity pay	20		305 (transfer)
Duty to consider flexible working	38 (one-off) 286 (recurring)		
Union learning reps	7 (year 1) 26 (year 8)		
Fixed term work	61 -136 (recurring)		

222.   The total one-off costs to employers of the changes proposed amount to £95-135 million. These reflect principally the costs of setting up disciplinary and grievance procedures and changes to personnel systems arising from paternity and adoption leave and pay and the duty to consider requests for flexible working from the parents of young children.

223.   Recurring costs to employers amount to £459-629 million. The principal costs arise from greater use of workplace procedures, covering for paternity and adoption leave and longer periods of maternity leave, supporting ULRs, and improving the pay and pensions of FTC employees. Costs will increase over time as ULRs become more widespread.

224.   The proposals also benefit employers. Many of these benefits - such as improved morale, skill utilisation and better employment relations - cannot be quantified. Some, however, have been quantified. These include recruitment savings from

more mothers returning to work after maternity leave, a reduction in costly Employment Tribunal cases, and greater productivity through ULRs. Initially, these benefits are quantified at £196-239 million. However, they will increase over time as ULRs become more widespread and more effective. It is possible that <u>quantified</u> benefits could exceed quantified costs to employers within a reasonable period of introduction - even leaving to one side the unquantified productivity benefits[5].

225.   Individual workers benefit by almost £453-527 million from enhanced maternity pay and paternity pay and adoption pay and improved pay and pensions for FTC employees. There are also modest financial benefits to individual applicants arising from the dispute resolution procedures that are roughly offset by costs arising from other elements in this package. But while this part of the Act may be broadly neutral in its financial effects, improved dispute resolution has broader but unquantified benefits.

226.   Costs to the taxpayer are expected to be around £380 million per year and arise almost entirely from maternity, paternity and adoption pay. The dispute resolution proposals should produce net savings to the taxpayer once the effect of the proposals has fed through into reduced Tribunal applications.

COMMENCEMENT

227.   There is a power for the Secretary of State to bring the provisions of the Act into force on such day as the Secretary of State may by order appoint, and different days may be so appointed for different purposes.

EUROPEAN CONVENTION ON HUMAN RIGHTS

228.   Section 19 of the Human Rights Act 1998 requires the Minister in charge of a Act in either House of Parliament to make a statement about the compatibility of the provisions of the Act with the Convention rights (as defined by section 1 of that Act). On 11th February 2002 Lord Sainsbury of Turville made the following statement:

229.   In my view the provisions of the Employment Act are compatible with the Convention rights.

HANSARD REFERENCES

230.   The following table sets out the dates and Hansard references for each stage of this Act's passage through Parliament.

---

[5] Using the range provided in the RIA for ULRs, total benefits to employers could be in the range £100-230 million after eight years.

Stage	Date	Hansard reference
House of Commons		
Introduction	8 November 2001	vol 374 cc 380
Second reading	27 November 2001	vol 375 cc 864-940
Committee	6 December 2001 – 24 January 2002	Hansard Standing Committee F
Report and Third reading	12 February 2002	vol 380 cc 79 - 180
House of Lords		
Introduction	13 February 2002	vol 631 cc 1138
Second reading	26 February 2002	vol 361 cc 1325-1341, 1356-1408
Grand Committee	13 March – 22 April 2002	vol 632 CWH 1-320, vol 633 CWH 321-518, vol 634 cc 519-550
Report	30 May –18 June 2002	vol 635 cc 1491-1568, vol 636 cc 135-252, 625-705
Third reading	27 June 2002	vol 636 cc 1522-1542

Royal Assent – 8 July 2002   House of Lords Hansard vol 637 col 554

GLOSSARY

Administration Act

The Social Security Administration Act 1992: the Act that contains most of the rules and regulation-making powers to specify how social security benefits should be claimed, paid and administered. It consolidated the existing legislation in 1992, and has been amended subsequently. See also the Social Security Contributions and Benefits Act 1992.

Advisory Conciliation and Arbitration Service

ACAS a permanent independent body - works to prevent and resolve employment disputes, conciliates in actual or potential complaints to employment tribunals, provides information and advice and promotes good practice.

ACAS Code of Practice on Discipline and Grievance Procedures

Gives employers practical advice on how to deal with disciplinary matters. Tribunals take into account any provision of the Code, which appears to them to be relevant to any question before them. They do not expect all employers to follow the Code to the letter regardless of their particular circumstances, but to decide to what extent it is practicable and necessary for an employer to do so given the size and administrative resources of his or her firm. Legislation specifically requires tribunals to take these factors into account when determining whether the employer acted reasonably.

Disability Discrimination Act 1995

The Disability Discrimination Act 1995 introduces, over a period of time, new laws and measures aimed at ending the discrimination faced by many people with disabilities. It gives disabled people new rights in employment, access to goods, facilities and services and the management, buying or renting of property.

Equal Pay Act 1970

The Equal Pay Act 1970 was introduced to make it unlawful to offer different pay and conditions where women and men are doing the same or like work or rated as equivalent in the same employment.

Equal Pay Directive

The Equal Pay Directive (75/117EC) requires employers to pay women the same pay as men for equal work or work of equal value, and is implemented in the UK to apply to all employers through the Equal Pay Act 1970 (as amended).

The Employment Appeal Tribunal Rules 1993 (SI 1993/2854) (as amended)

The rules contain provisions relating to proceedings before the EAT, including on the institution of appeals, attendance of witnesses and production of documents, oral hearings, hearings in private and drawing up orders disposing of appeals.

Employment Rights Act 1996

These and other provisions relating to individual employment rights were consolidated into the Employment Rights Act 1996, bringing them together in a more concise and readily accessible form. A number of amendments have been made to the 1996 Act, principally by the Employment Relations Act 1999.

Employment Tribunals Act 1996

This Act contains provisions relating to the constitution, powers and procedure of employment tribunals and the Employment Appeal Tribunal.

Employment Tribunals Rules of Procedure

The rules governing the procedure of employment tribunals in Great Britain, made under powers in the Employment Tribunals Act 1996, and set out in the Employment Tribunals (Constitution and Rules of Procedure) Regulations 2001 (SI 2001/1171) and the Employment Tribunals (Constitution and Rules of Procedure) (Scotland) Regulations 2001 (SI 2001/1170).

Expected week of confinement (EWC)

The week containing the date on which the woman expects to be confined. Confined means labour resulting in child born alive or labour after 24 weeks of pregnancy resulting in the birth of a child alive or dead.

Employment Relations Act 1999

The provisions of this Act form part of a package of reforms to employment and trade union law outlined in the Government's White Paper, *Fairness at Work*, published in May 1998.

Human Rights Act 1998

An Act to give further effect to rights and freedoms guaranteed under the European Convention on Human Rights

Incapacity Benefit (IB)

A taxable contributory benefit introduced in April 1995 to replace Sickness and Invalidity Benefits for people who are unable to work because of illness or disability. Payable weekly at 1 of 3 rates:

- a short-term lower rate: payable to those who do not qualify for Statutory Sick Pay, for the first 28 weeks of incapacity

- a short-term higher rate: payable from 28 weeks to 52 weeks of incapacity

- a long-term rate: payable after 52 weeks of incapacity

Income Support (IS)

An income-related (means-tested) benefit for people who are not in work (or working less than 16 hours a week) and whose income is less than a specified level. It is calculated on the basis of age, family membership and other prescribed circumstances.

Invalid Care Allowance (ICA)

A non-contributory, non-means-tested benefit for people who give up the opportunity of full-time work to provide care on a regular and substantial basis (at least 35 hours or more a week) to a severely disabled person.

Jobseeker's Act 1995

The Act that introduced Jobseeker's Allowance.

Jobseeker's Allowance (JSA)

Jobseeker's Allowance is the social security benefit for people who are unemployed or who are working for less than 16 hours per week. To qualify for JSA a jobseeker must be capable of work, available for work, actively seeking work, and must enter into a "Jobseeker's Agreement" which sets out the steps he will take in order to find work. Jobseekers who have paid sufficient National Insurance contributions can receive contribution-based JSA at a personal rate for up to six months. Those who do not qualify for contribution-based JSA, or whose needs are not met by the contribution-based allowance, can claim income-based JSA for themselves and their dependants subject to a means test. Income-based JSA is paid for as long as needed, provided that the qualifying conditions continue to be met.

Lower Earnings Limit (LEL)

The level of earnings at which people secure entitlement to contributory benefits. Weekly earnings above this point (and up to the Upper Earnings Limit) accrue entitlement to SERPS or to contracted-out rebates. Employee National Insurance contributions are payable on earnings above the Primary Threshold, which is also the Income Tax Personal Allowance, up to the Upper Earnings Limit. However, for contributory benefit purposes, National Insurance contributions are treated as paid on earnings between the Lower Earnings Limit and the Primary Threshold.

Maternity Allowance (MA)

Maternity Allowance is paid to certain women who do not qualify for Statutory Maternity Pay, to the self-employed, and to recently employed women. To qualify, they must have been employed or self-employed in at least 26 of the 66 weeks (the test period) ending with the week before the Expected Week of Confinement (EWC). There are two rates of MA. Women whose average earnings are at least equal to the Lower Earnings Limit in force at the beginning of their test period receive standard rate MA. Women whose average earnings are below that Lower Earnings Limit but at least £30 receive 90% of their average weekly earnings (subject to a £62.20 maximum).

National Insurance contributions

Contributions payable by those in work and their employer into the National Insurance fund, which are used to pay contributory social security benefits to qualifying individuals. Self-employed people pay a lower rate but have more limited rights to benefits.

New Deal

New Deal is a key part of the Government's Welfare to Work strategy. It has been created to help unemployed people into work by closing the gap between the skills employers want and the skills people can offer.

Partner

"Partner" means a person who is a member of the same couple as the claimant.

PAYE

Stands for 'Pay As You Earn'. Most people pay income tax under this system. Under PAYE, employers take tax from weekly or monthly earnings and pay it over to the Inland Revenue.

Race Relations Act 1976

An Act that made provisions with respect to discrimination on racial grounds and relations between people of different racial groups.

Sex Discrimination Act 1975

An Act that renders unlawful certain kinds of sex discrimination and discrimination on the grounds of marriage, and establishing a Commission with the function of working towards the elimination of such discrimination and promoting equality of opportunity between men and women.

Social Security Contributions and Benefits Act 1992

The Social Security Contributions and Benefits Act 1992: contains most of the provisions for setting out the rules for National Insurance Contributions and entitlement to social security benefits (with the exception of Jobseeker's Allowance). It consolidated the existing legislation when it was introduced in 1992, and has been amended since then. Several sections of this Act have their effect by amending it. See also the Administration Act.

Social Security Act 1998

Provided for a new system for making decisions on cases and handling disputes and appeals.

Statutory Sick Pay

Statutory Sick Pay is administered by the employer, up to a period of 28 weeks, if the employee has been sick for at least 4 consecutive days (including weekends and bank holidays), and if the employee earns enough on average for it to be relevant for National Insurance purposes. Cases of dispute are dealt with by the Inland Revenue.

Statutory Maternity Pay (SMP)

Statutory Maternity Pay is paid to pregnant employees (or those who have given birth) who satisfy two basic tests. A woman must have been employed continuously by her employer for at least 26 weeks into the 15th week before the expected week of confinement (EWC); and she must earn on average at or above the Lower Earnings Limit (LEL) (currently £72 a week). There are two weekly rates. The higher rate is 90% of the employee's average weekly earnings and is payable for the first six weeks for which SMP is payable. The lower rate is a standard rate (currently £62.20) which is reviewed annually and is payable for the remaining weeks of the Maternity Pay Period.

Tax Credits Act 1999

An Act to provide for family credit and disability working allowance to be known, respectively, as working families' tax credit and disabled person's tax credit; and to make

64

further provision with respect to those credits, including provision for the transfer of functions relating to them.

Trade Union and Labour Relations (Consolidation) Act 1992

Brings together all collective employment rights including trade union finances and elections; union members' rights including dismissal, time off; redundancy consultation; ACAS, CAC and CROTUM; industrial action legislation. Does not cover individual rights like unfair dismissal, redundancy pay, maternity etc (these are covered by 1978 EPCA)

Upper Earnings Limit

The level of weekly earnings above which there is no liability for employee National Insurance contributions. It sets the upper limit for the weekly earnings on which SERPS accrue and which qualify for contracted-out rebates. See also Lower Earnings Limit.

Welfare Reform and Pensions Act 1999

Introduced a range of measures relating to Social Security benefits (including the introduction of Work-focused interviews), pensions and National Insurance contributions.

Working Families' Tax Credits

A tax credit payable to working families depending on their circumstances, which has replaced Family Credit and is administered by the Inland Revenue, and is paid through the pay packet.

Printed in the UK by The Stationery Office Limited
under the authority and superintendence of Carol Tullo, Controller of
Her Majesty's Stationery Office and Queen's Printer of Acts of Parliament